Carpentry

BY WALTER IAN FISCHMAN

GROSSET
GOOD LIFE
BOOKS

PUBLISHERS · GROSSET & DUNLAP · NEW YORK
A FILMWAYS COMPANY

Acknowledgments

Cover photograph by Mort Engel

The author wishes to express his appreciation to the following for permission to use their illustrations: Anderson Cork Co.: p. 74 top left, p. 74 top right, p. 74 middle left, p. 74 middle right, p. 74 bottom right, p. 75; Armstrong Cork Co.: p. 69, p. 70; BernzOmatic Inc.: p. 93 right; Black & Decker: p. 36, p. 39, p. 40, p. 122; California Redwood Assn.: p. 44 bottom, p. 50, p. 51, p. 65, p. 67, p. 68, p. 71, p. 72, p. 74 bottom left, p. 76; Crescent: p. 25 bottom left, p. 25 bottom, p. 25 bottom right, p. 29 bottom right, p. 30 bottom left, p. 30 bottom, p. 31 bottom, p. 99 top right; Cross & Blackwell: p. 99 bottom; Elmco: p. 107; Hand Tools Institute: p. 28, p. 126; Home Tool Institute: p. 9; Peter Kalberkamp: p. 7 bottom, p. 18, p. 118; Lloyd Lumber Co.: p. 115, p. 116; Lufkin: p. 25 top, p. 32 top, p. 32; Nicholson: p. 20 middle right, p. 20 bottom lower, p. 21 top left, p. 21 top right, p. 22 bottom right, p. 85 middle; Gerald Pfeifer: p. 10; Rockwell International: p. 34 top, p. 35, p. 37, p. 39 bottom left; Daniel S. Roher, Inc.: p. 29 top; Rohm & Haas Co.: p. 110, p. 111, p. 112, p. 113; Royal Glass Co.: p. 63; Stanley Works: p. 20 top, p. 20 top lower, p. 20 middle left, p. 21 middle, p. 21 bottom, p. 22 top left, p. 22 top right, p. 22 bottom left, p. 23, p. 24, p. 25 middle, p. 26, p. 29 middle upper left, p. 29 middle lower left, p. 29 middle right, p. 29 lower left, p. 29 bottom, p. 30 top left, p. 30 top right, p. 30 middle upper, p. 30 middle lower, p. 34 bottom, p. 38, p. 41 top, p. 48, p. 62, p. 81 bottom right, p. 85 top, p. 88 bottom, p. 89, p. 92 right, p. 93 left, p. 98 bottom right, p. 99 top left, p. 99 top, p. 101 right, p. 102 middle, p. 102 bottom, p. 104, p. 123; Teco: p. 46 top, p. 46 middle, p. 46 bottom, p. 47 top, p. 47 middle, p. 47 bottom, p. 58, p. 59, p. 66; U.S. Plywood Co.: p. 45, p. 46 right, p. 47 left; Kal Wegner: p. 55 top; Western Wood Products Assn.: p. 4, p. 6, p. 7 top left, p. 7 middle, p. 7 right, p. 44 top, p. 49, p. 52 top, p. 52 bottom left, p. 53; Xcerlite: p. 29 middle, p. 30 bottom right, p. 31 top, p. 31 middle, p. 100.

The Stanley Tool Guide, copyright © 1968: p. 13, p. 14, p. 15, p. 16, p. 17, p. 41 bottom, p. 55 bottom left, p. 60, p. 79, p. 81 top, p. 81 middle, p. 81 bottom left, p. 82, p. 83, p. 84, p. 85 bottom, p. 86, p. 87, p. 88 top, p. 88 middle, p. 90, p. 91, p. 92 left, p. 94, p. 95, p. 96, p. 97, p. 98 bottom left, p. 101 left, p. 102 top, p. 120, p. 121, p. 124, p. 125.

Sources of Plans

Stanley Tools
195 Lake Street
New Britain, Connecticut 06050

Western Wood Products Association
700 Yeon Building
Portland, Oregon 97204

Contents

To get a teenager to put his things away, you have to provide him with something besides a floor or a bed to put them on. Making this handsome and useful combination desk, shelving, and cabinet is not as complicated as it looks. Favored belongings and decorations also go along with a study center, and the carpenter can alter the plans to fit the needs of the student, and get him to act as carpenter's assistant. (See Acknowledgments page for source of detailed plans.)

1
Two Kinds of Carpenters

For the purposes of this book, there are two kinds of carpenters. There's the recreational carpenter who makes things to add to the fun of life, such as a deck or a "crow's nest" for a child's room, or toy shelves or a large indoor wood or plastic planter (plastic being just like wood so far as carpentry goes).

Being a recreational carpenter saves a great deal of expense, because you can get what you want for a fraction of what the article would cost if you purchased it. The recreational carpenter can buy parts that he is not equipped to make, such as turned legs for a piece of furniture.

The other kind of carpenter is the one with some degree of skill and some equipment. In the face of higher costs, you may want to read up on how-to-do-it and do-it-yourself with a helper, or you may want to hire a carpenter and be his helper. And, above all, you may want to seek professional design help from an architect.

Whether adding on to a room, building a new wall in the house, putting in a new floor over an old one, or installing a door or window, home carpentry is both a dollar-saving device and a means of extending the good life.

You can learn from this book what you need to know about wood, about construction, about making picture-frames, about creating something for your husband or wife or children. Most of all, you can become acquainted with the basic tools you need and how to use them. There is some expense involved, but nothing like the expense of purchasing the finished product. This book describes not only how to handle the household screwdriver or hammer, but also how to use a carpenter's level to make your wall straight and how to use hand-tools, whether the less expensive hand-saw or the infinitely faster hand power-saw. There are, in fact, only about four basic power-tools needed by the home carpenter for large projects. You will find the fully equipped workshop does not require a major investment, but a modest one. And you will find here the plans for making over an entire room that can be built with little effort using the right saw and nails and prefab concrete piers. The day of the big spender is over; the day of the maker is here.

In the following chapter, we will show the basic hand-tools that a home carpenter can begin to collect. When you are ready to begin a project, such as a backyard bench or louvered fence, turn to the later chapter on How to Use

Landscape structures

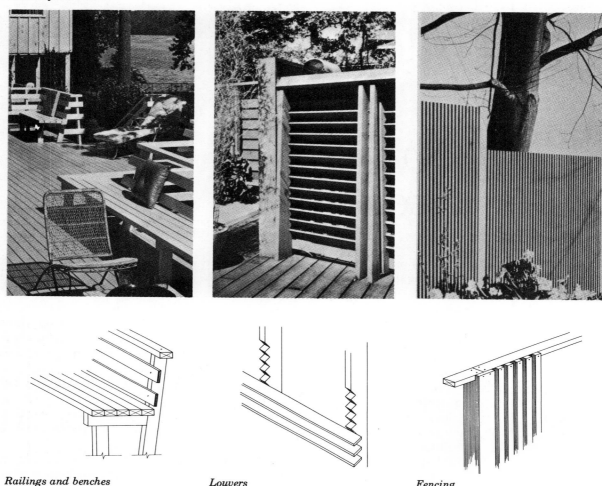

Railings and benches   *Louvers*   *Fencing*

Hand-tools, where you will find a thorough discussion of how to handle your tools and maintain them.

Before you get into basic carpentry, here are a few samples of simple things that you might want to make, with suggestions for ways of constructing them.

Writing Desk

The beginning carpenter can achieve excellent results speedily with prefabricated parts, as shown in the design here for a writing desk. It involved very little carpentry, yet it is attractive, personalized, and useful. The drawers, including one file drawer (usually not available in most home desks), can be obtained from a hardware store or from an unpainted wood furniture shop.

The desk top can be a solid flush door, or plywood of ⅝- to 1-inch width, or anything else that can serve effectively as a base for a glass top. Get rather heavy glass from a glazier — at least ¼-inch — cut to fit the desk top precisely, with corners rounded and edges polished.

To personalize the desk, cloth or paper objects can be inserted under the glass: memorabilia of a trip, including maps, tickets, postcards (even foreign coins or unusual hotel receipts); or favorite prints, such as drawings of American scenes or engravings of military costumes. One family filled the space with several generations of photos, some going back to tintype days, of family relatives.

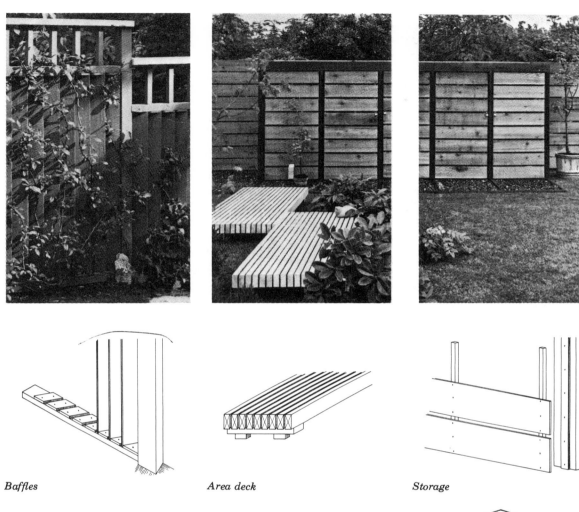

Baffles   *Area deck*   *Storage*

The legs for such a desk — and several members of the family may wish desks of different sizes or styles for their own rooms — can be purchased at a hardware store in metal or wood, and fitted to the precise height of the drawers using wood blocks screwed into the underside of the desk. Leg braces can be obtained for both metal and wood legs. Drawer-pulls are available in a wide variety of styles to suit different decors, and the file drawer can be fitted with metal "hangers" for file folders. It's great for school papers as well as for family documents, bills, receipts, etc. All parts of the desk, except the glass top, can be painted to blend with whatever pictures or designs are used under the glass tops. Heavy acrylic plastic tops can be used in place of glass.

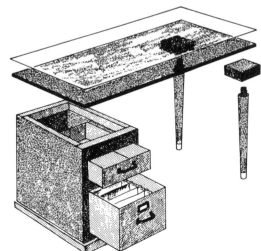

A personalized writing desk

2
Some Advice on Tools

Unless you have been able to find the best workman and were willing to pay the painful cost, you have had to do some occasional fast fix-it or build-it projects to keep your walls from collapsing about your ears. In the process you may have been painfully aware of that old adage, "It's a poor workman who blames his tools."

All very well, but that saying is only half true.

Granted, it is easy to blame the saw when you haven't cut straight or to pin the onus on the hammer when it's your right arm (unskilled, of course) that's really at fault. But there is another side to this situation.

It is very tough to do a decent, workmanlike job using badly made or inefficient tools. The solution is simple. Before you become involved in this sort of home activity, tool up for the work. Acquire an assortment of efficient, good-quality, well-designed tools that enable you to use all the skills you can muster.

Tools for What Purpose?

Homeowners need tools for different purposes. It's important to know just which category you fit into, because it will determine the type and number of tools you should buy. For example, if you do not intend to tackle anything more than a few minor fix-it jobs about the house, it makes no sense to spend money on a toolshop with a vast array of hardware, most of which will probably never be used.

Your carpentry exploits might be restricted to such quick and easy tasks as hanging pictures, tightening doorknobs, putting up windowshades, and replacing a broken board. For work of this nature you probably won't need more than a lightweight hammer, a couple of screwdrivers, a pair of pliers, and a hand-saw.

But the cost of living may demand that you go in for small building projects or larger-scale repair jobs. In this event, you need a decent hammer with a nail-set, a crosscut saw and a ripsaw, a level, an adjustable wrench, and perhaps a small hand-drill (the eggbeater variety will do quite nicely — see page 23), together with a small assortment of drill-bits. In addition, you will probably find at

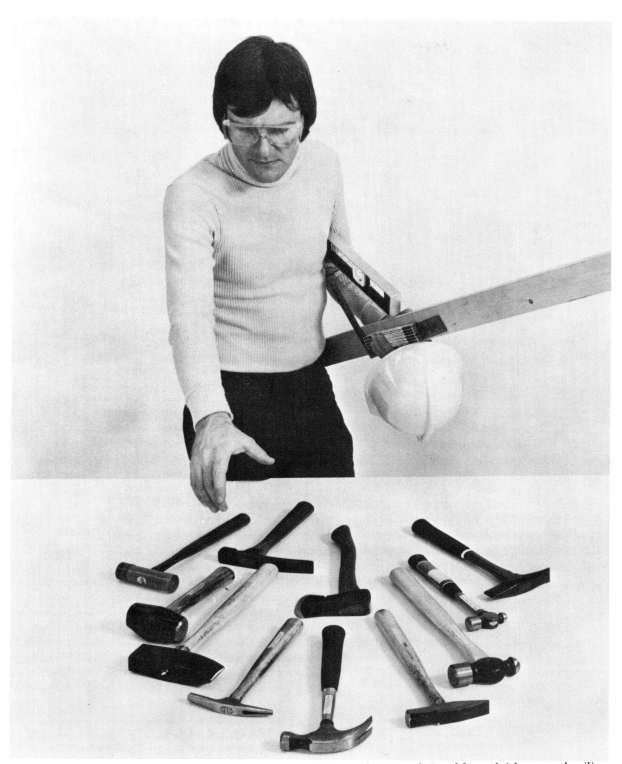

Which hammer should you choose? Hammers shown are designed for such jobs as wood-nailing, masonry-nailing and drilling, splitting bricks, splitting wood, and driving stakes.

least two types of screwdrivers necessary (see page 24).

In the heady altitudes of major construction and remodeling projects, the necessary equipment verges on the assortment used by a professional carpenter, including power-tools. But if you are easing into this, you will want to choose carefully from the lists on the following pages.

There is one more classification, and this one cuts loose from the restrictions of logic or need. If you have contracted a case of that very popular home-workshop fever, you may find that you have developed an intense longing for tools and hardware that by any logical reasoning you don't really need. You yearn for these items and don't rest easy until you have acquired them. If you have been hit by this malady, there's only one treatment. Relax and enjoy it.

The Tool Kit

Plan to build the assortment of tools in your kit slowly. And *kit* means just that — a small metal toolbox scientifically designed to hold the small tools that even the most professional carpenter needs. It fastens like an enlarged

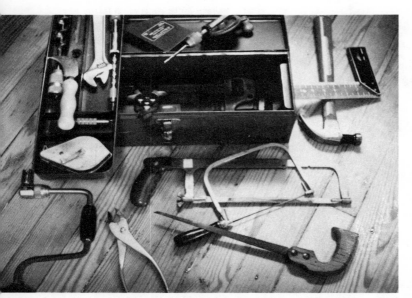

A homeowner's tool-kit of well-worn tools, a display of all that is needed to fit into an 18x6-inch tool-kit. The larger tools such as a crosscut saw, ripsaw, and jack-plane are, of course, not here.

lunchbox, and can be lugged up ladders and kept at hand when larger tools cannot. It will hold a keyhole saw and a coping saw, a hammer and a chisel, but nothing larger. And the average healthy person can easily handle it. Don't underestimate its usefulness.

A Major Project

If major construction is necessary, and if the funds are not available to hire professional help, an amateur can — with careful study and judicious investment — jump in with both feet. One person I know did just that — converted a summer cottage into a charming home for a growing family. But he took the one necessary precaution — he made careful plans with an architect, and he followed the plans precisely. This book is not intended for such ambitious carpentry. Rather, it is a word of caution for the person who goes overboard easily.

The Beginner

Most people can and should invest in a few basic tools at the start (see Chapter 3). Carefully and wisely sort out the tools you already have. Throw away the damaged ones that could wreck your work, such as a dented chisel. Then, one or two at a time, pick up additional tools as you need them. It is hard to predict in advance just which items will be required, because you may not know what the carpentry job will require next. You need not wind up with expensive gadgetry gracing the tool rack.

Learning with Your Tools

If you acquire your tools a few at a time, you will have the opportunity to learn how to use each one on a reasonable time-schedule. To become familiar with them, you should practice or take a carpentry course or study the chapter How to Use Hand-tools. Freed of urgency, the learning process is fun. On a speeded-up basis, it is frequently a nightmare of mistakes.

The Signs of Quality

There are a few signs of quality that serve as a general guide to the purchase of tools. First, there is the type of metal that is used to make the tool. It may take an engineering degree to know metal really well, but there are some points of knowledge that you can acquire easily.

When high-quality metal of the proper type has been used in the tool, this information is generally stamped or printed somewhere on the tool. For example, if you are buying a pair of pliers, the best will have the words "drop forged" etched or stamped into the metal. It's the manufacturer's way of saying, "I used the best possible ingredients to make this tool." So always examine all surfaces carefully to spot these pride-in-workmanship announcements. Inferior tools do not bear such markings.

Almost invariably, good tools are made more carefully than shoddy ones, so examine each tool carefully. In purchasing tools, you should make sure that there are no raw unfinished edges especially on the working surfaces of the tool. For example, the jaws of a pair of pliers should meet perfectly and evenly. Hold the tool up to the light for a fast and easy test. There should be no excess metal from the casting process. But don't be misled by chrome-plating. This may be used to add flashy sales appeal.

As a matter of fact, you may run across tools that take a sort of homespun approach to appearance. The jaws and working parts of a pair of pliers or a wrench may be beautifully machined and polished, while the nonworking parts of the tool — the handles, the back-surfaces of the jaws — may be relatively rough and crude. It's the manufacturer's way of saying, "I've designed and manufactured this tool inexpensively to do an honest hard day's work. It's not pretty *but* it will serve you well."

Cheap Tools

Unhappily, cost is an almost direct indicator of quality. Good tools cost more than bad tools, and sometimes they cost a great deal more. For example, for a dollar or less, you can pick up a screwdriver that looks perfectly serviceable, and yet the first time you try to use it, the shaft will come loose from the handle, the metal at the tip will bend, or the tip will refuse to seat properly in the slot in the screw. Nothing can be more frustrating or wasteful.

By contrast, a good screwdriver might sell for several dollars. Such a tool won't fall apart, and will fit the job for which it was intended.

Where to Buy Tools

A storekeeper soon learns whether you are going to become a steady customer. If it seems likely that you will be, it's sound business for the manager to guide you carefully in your selection. If you find a store where they take pride in their stock of tools, know the individual items well, and are interested in their regular customers, you will probably receive good guidance.

But make sure they know you live in the neighborhood and shop in their area regularly. Tell them the extent of the job you want to tackle. The whole routine comes down to some basic aspects of economics. If they want to see you come walking through the front door time and time again, or if you establish a charge account, they will treat you well and carefully.

The Handiest Tool for You

A final point is an intangible one. For any tool to be a good one for you, it has to feel right in your hand. Your own physical strength has much to do with this. There are no rules for "feel" and no meaningful guidelines. You probably won't understand it until you have done a fair amount of carpentry work, but a tool that doesn't feel right in your hand is like an unwanted neighbor. You learn to live with it, but you would prefer it to be intangibly different. Perhaps it's the balance, the shape of the handle, the weight, whatever. So heft and handle tools at the store before making your selection. Some stores will even allow you to return a tool that you don't like if it's in its original undamaged state.

Bargains

To avoid headaches, avoid certain types of bargains. Don't confuse these with legitimate bargains. In order to increase business, stores may sometimes have sales on tools or they may reduce certain items they are closing out.

However, some tools are manufactured specifically to be sold at bargain rates. They look good. They may even be replicas of standard-brand tools, and yet they sell for a fraction of the regular price. But their shiny exterior is generally a guarantee that you will have workshop woes you can do without.

Used Tools

Surprisingly enough, used tools may be a bargain — as long as you can judge the quality. For some work, even professional carpenters prefer used tools. In recent years, metallurgy has changed and modern hammer-heads are made of harder steel. The face or striking surface of an old used hammer-head is frequently slightly dented from the impact of thousands of blows striking nail-heads, and some carpenters prize such hammer-heads highly because they have less of a tendency to skitter off the nail when they're made of slightly softer metal. But stay away from badly battered tools. Why rejuvenate a tool long past its prime, files that are dull, or screwdriver blades butchered beyond use?

Don't be afraid of a little rust in used tools. There are excellent rust-dissolving compounds you can use to restore old tools.

Gadgets

For the most part, stay away from gadgets. The handy-dandy combination-tool fits into this category — the screwdriver with an awkward assortment of unrelated parts telescoped into the handle, a tack-lifter, and maybe a miniature sawblade. Save your money. If you want to hammer a nail, buy a hammer. If you want to drive a screw, buy a screwdriver.

Legitimate Double-Duty Tools

It's entirely possible for some tools to serve double duty. For example, hand-saws are made with either straight or curved backs. If you buy one with a straight back, you can easily use it as a straight-edge to mark a guideline for sawing the board.

As you become a more experienced carpenter, you will probably also acquire your own assortment of improvised tools. Some of these can be highly effective. For example, many home-handymen swear by a beer-can opener for digging out plaster along the line of a cracked wall, before patching the crack.

Learn to extend the use of the tools you have. Once you have a working knowledge of a tool, you can adapt it for oddball situations. For example, if you have to pull a nail whose head is broken off just above the surface of the wood, you can grasp the little nub with the jaws of a self-locking plier wrench, then fit the claw of your hammer underneath the wrench and draw out the nail.

Brand-Names

There is one more guidepost to quality that will help you in your selection. Buy tools made by reputable companies whose names you recognize, firms who've been in business for a considerable length of time. They are likely to be around in the years to come. Since they have a reputation to maintain, they will avoid fast-buck procedures and introducing shoddy tools under their highly regarded brand-name. Granted, in this day of tough marketing, this is not always an infallible guide.

In the next two chapters, which are illustrated and contain brief descriptions, you will find a list of twenty-three tools that you are likely to need around your apartment or house. Authorities differ on how many are necessary, just as householders will differ. One major tool company lists twenty-four and a workbench.

Some of the tools we have selected as Primary are very familiar — such as the monkey-wrench, which carpenters call an adjustable wrench — but some may surprise you. Many a home-carpenter thinks there is only one kind of saw that he is likely to use, without knowing the difference between a crosscut saw and a ripsaw.

Twenty-three sounds like a lot of tools, but if you are used to making repairs at all, you may already own many of them. What you don't know is that with them you can construct a wide variety of useful objects and that many of these objects can be made quite easily.

Some of these objects may be things you have wanted but could not find in local stores, or you may have thought them too expensive for the use you would get out of them. We have tried to include a wide variety of home carpentry projects.

You will find here the simple homey objects that you can make in a short time. Others will seem beyond your ability, but you may be able to adjust the plan or you may decide to tackle the problem after buying a tool that will permit you to make it and many other objects like it.

Some of the following plans, such as that for

the black-and-gold mirror framed with decorative columns, are really prefab adaptations. Where turned legs or turned posts in half-raised mounting are needed, they can be purchased inexpensively. Cut in half, these turned posts or legs can provide you with any number of decorative devices that might seem totally impossible to achieve otherwise.

Basic house construction is described in later chapters.

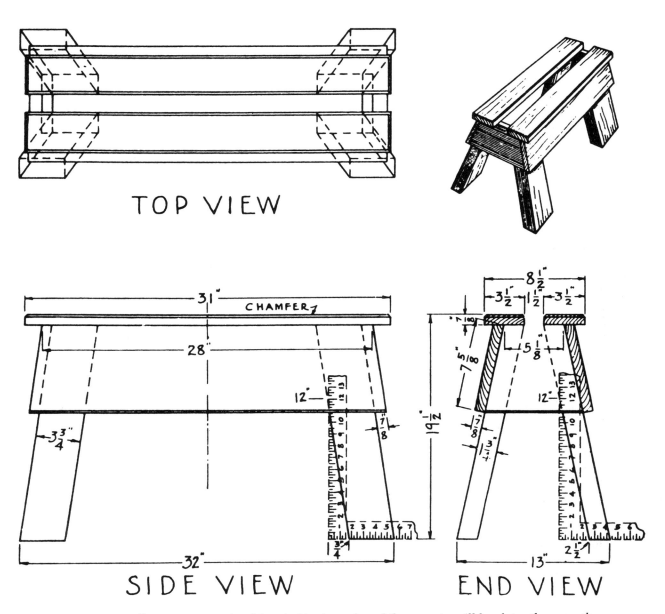

TOP VIEW

SIDE VIEW

END VIEW

For any carpentry involving sizable pieces of wood the carpenter will knock together a rough sawhorse, rather than trying to bridge chairs and the like. After the job, the sawhorse can be knocked apart.

Card and game table with preturned legs, prepurchased

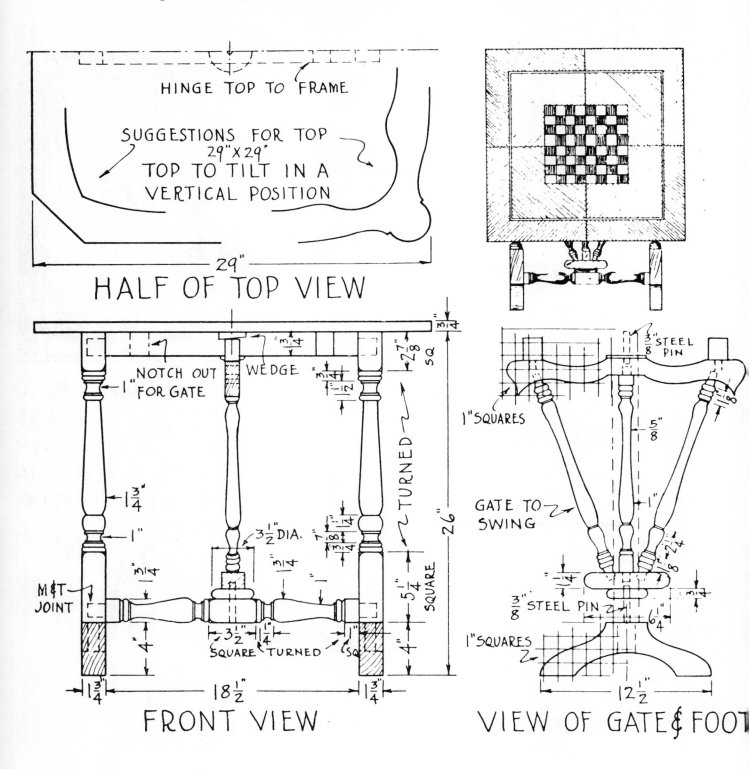

HINGE TOP TO FRAME

SUGGESTIONS FOR TOP
29" x 29"
TOP TO TILT IN A
VERTICAL POSITION

29"

HALF OF TOP VIEW

NOTCH OUT FOR GATE

WEDGE

1"

$1\frac{3}{4}$

1"

$3\frac{1}{2}$" DIA.

M&T JOINT

$\frac{3}{4}$

4"

$3\frac{1}{2}$" SQUARE

$1\frac{1}{4}$" TURNED

$\frac{3}{4}$"

1"

4"

$\frac{3}{4}$"

$1\frac{3}{4}$

$18\frac{1}{2}$"

$1\frac{3}{4}$

$2\frac{7}{8}$"

$\frac{3}{4}$" SQ.

TURNED

$5\frac{1}{4}$" SQUARE

26"

FRONT VIEW

$\frac{3}{8}$" STEEL PIN

1" SQUARES

$\frac{5}{8}$

GATE TO SWING

1"

$\frac{1}{4}$

$\frac{3}{8}$" STEEL PIN

$\frac{3}{4}$

$8\frac{1}{4}$"

$6\frac{1}{4}$"

1" SQUARES

$12\frac{1}{2}$"

VIEW OF GATE & FOOT

Black-and-gold mirror, with prepurchased columns

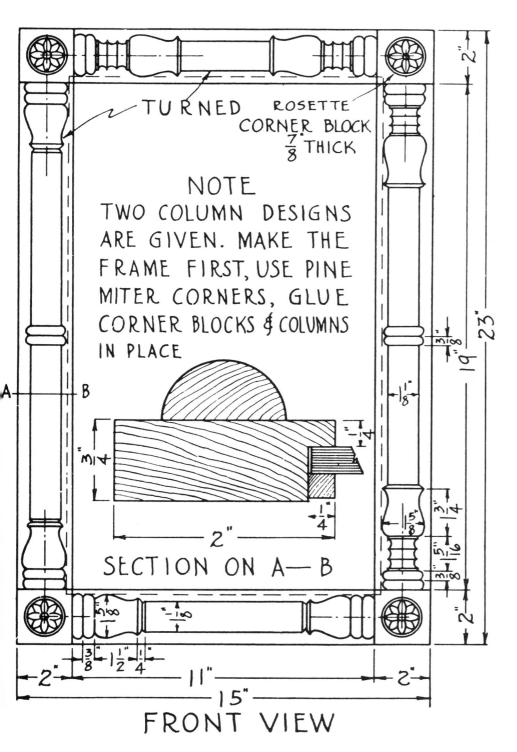

TURNED

ROSETTE
CORNER BLOCK
$\frac{7}{8}$" THICK

NOTE
TWO COLUMN DESIGNS
ARE GIVEN. MAKE THE
FRAME FIRST, USE PINE
MITER CORNERS, GLUE
CORNER BLOCKS & COLUMNS
IN PLACE

A — B

SECTION ON A—B

FRONT VIEW

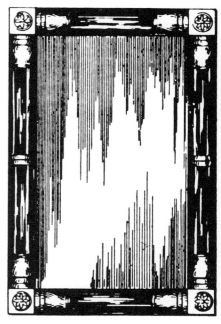

FINISH FRAME IN A
FLAT BLACK OIL PAINT
WITH GOLD CORNER
BLOCKS, COLUMNS IN
BLACK & OLD GOLD

Bird feeding-box

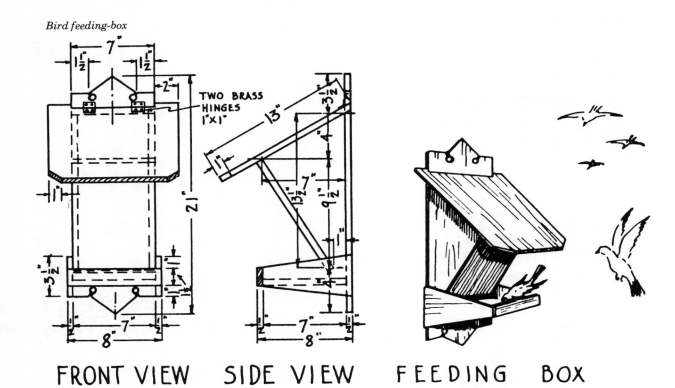

FRONT VIEW   SIDE VIEW   FEEDING BOX

Wren house

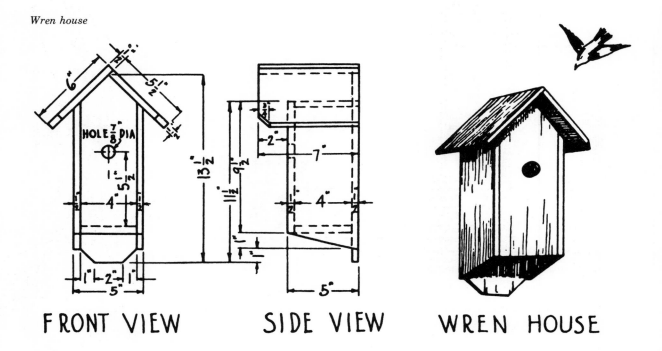

FRONT VIEW   SIDE VIEW   WREN HOUSE

Adirondack chair

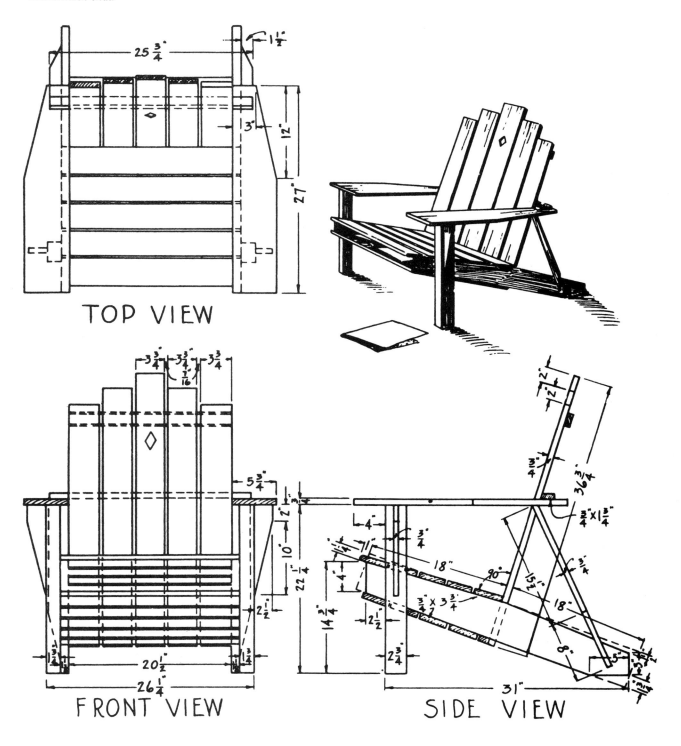

TOP VIEW

FRONT VIEW

SIDE VIEW

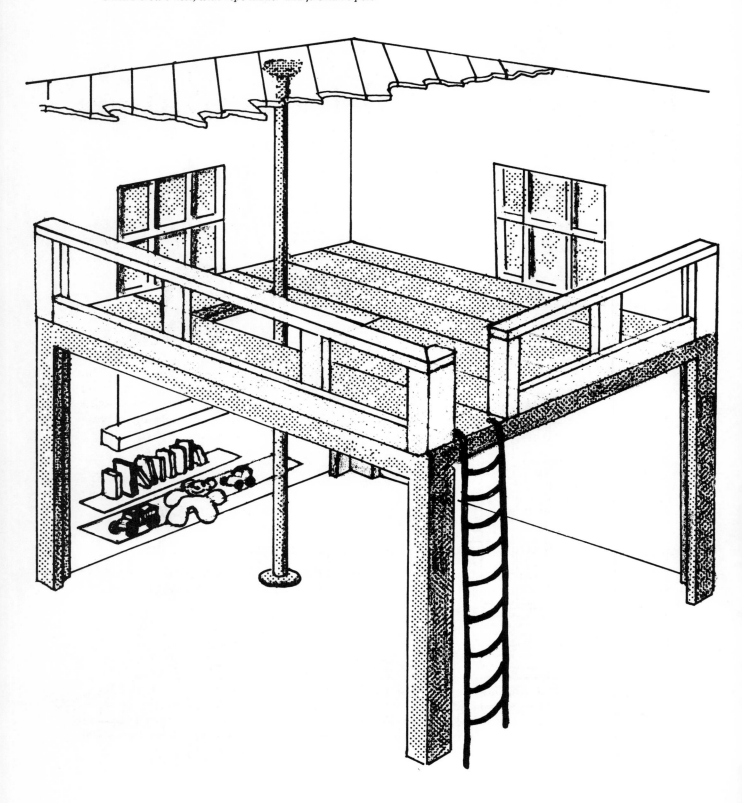

Child's crow's-nest, with rope ladder and fireman's pole

3
Primary Hand-tools and How to Select Them

The most important consideration in assembling home workshop tools is that they fit the types of jobs you want to do. The great range of selections available is enough to hassle a computer. To ease the confusion, we will list the most essential ones for any household. (For How to Use Hand-tools, see Chapter 10.)

Hammers

Curved-claw Hammer

For most general work, buy a 16-ounce curved-claw hammer. That 16-ounce figure refers to the weight of the head. Usually, the 16-ounce variety is just the proper heft for an average home-carpenter to swing comfortably over an average working period. Some men and women might select a lighter weight. Generally, hammer-head weights range from 7 ounces (suitable for driving tacks) all the way up to 28 ounces (fine for pounding spikes).

Ripping Hammer

At the hardware store you will see another variety with a straight claw. The most important straight-claw hammer for the home-carpenter is a ripping hammer. A straight-claw hammer is used for general carpentry work.

Nail-set

Just as the name indicates, the nail-set is used to drive or set the head of finishing-nails slightly below the surface of the wood. (For types of nails, see Chapter 11.)

Saws

Crosscut Saw

A crosscut saw is designed to cut with ease across or perpendicular to the grain of wood. The teeth of a crosscut are alternately slanted to one side of the blade and then the other. This gives two rows of teeth so that the cut is wider than the thickness of the blade, thereby keeping the saw from binding or sticking in the cut.

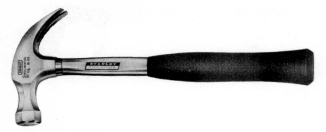

Curved-claw hammer

Ripping hammer

Nail-set

Ripsaw

Again, the name is the tip-off. The teeth of the ripsaw are designed to cut parallel to the grain of the wood, to rip boards into long strips. The teeth have much less "set" or spread to them than the teeth of the crosscut saw, but they are coarser.

Keyhole Saw

The fine-tipped blade got its name because it was once actually used to cut keyholes. It is intended for sawing within narrow spaces.

Coping Saw

One of the most popular tools around the family is the coping saw. The thin blades are easy to insert, and thin pieces of wood can be cut in innumerable shapes, like a jigsaw puzzle. If you have no hacksaw, the coping saw can be used with a special blade for cutting metal.

Hacksaw

The hacksaw is the toughie among small saws, with carbon blades and with some even tougher, to cut through pipe, stubborn bolts, and other metal too thick for any other hand-tool to get through.

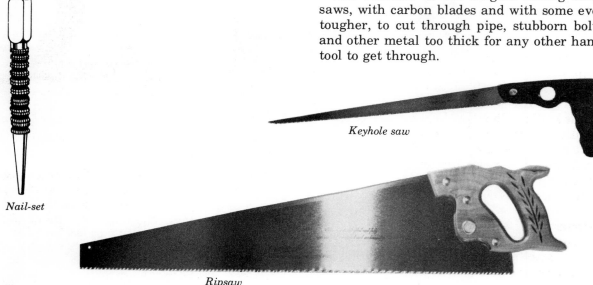

Keyhole saw

Ripsaw

Crosscut saw

Coping saw

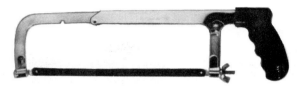
Hacksaw

Miter Box and Backsaw

For cutting precise angles in wood, you can hardly do without a miter box and its backsaw, which has a wide blade and fine teeth. For the amateur, it's almost impossible to make an accurate picture-frame corner in any other way.

Safety

This is as good a place as any, after describing saws, to remind you that you should take a few safety and convenience measures even with hand-tools.

Eye-protector

If you are chipping metal or doing light grinding, there's always a danger that the fragments may fly loose and lodge in your eye. Clear plastic safety goggles can end this hazard. (See Chapter 10.) Incidentally, the industrial safety regulations in a good many states make it mandatory that professional craftsmen wear eye-protectors (as well as breathing masks) when tackling dangerous grinding or metal-working jobs.

Gloves

It seems silly to mention, but an amateur can save himself a good many cuts and blisters if he uses ordinary workman's gloves. They'll be a hindrance sometimes, but that's a matter of judgment.

Carpenter's Apron

To save many trips up and down ladders for small tools or for nails of various sizes, pocketed aprons made of canvas are a convenience more necessary in woodwork than aprons are in the kitchen.

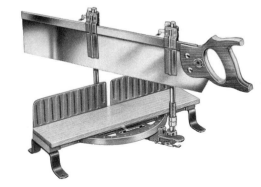
Miter box and backsaw

Jack-plane

Wood-planes

Planes come in lengths from 4 to 22 inches, and all are intended to smooth wood surfaces, such as the edges of boards, and to fit wood, such as door edges. The longer the plane, the truer the straight-edge.

Jack-plane

The jack-plane, 12 to 15 inches long, is the most common.

Block-plane

The shortest plane, usually about 6 inches long, is the block-plane. It can be held and used in one hand, and is quite versatile, but it cannot be expected to make long surfaces perfectly level.

Block-plane

Wood-chisel

Chisels

Wood-chisel

Limit your selection to chisels made with metal or plastic handles. You can push these by hand or you can hit them with any type of hammer and not get into trouble. The most popular length is the one with a blade of about 4 to 5 inches.

Stick to the type of tool called a *firmer-chisel*. The blade will be a little thicker than the type designed primarily for cabinet-work. In width, chisels range from ⅛ inch to 1 to 2 inches.

Don't buy more than two chisels — ½ and 1 inch. Pick up additional ones as you need them.

Cold-chisel

Stubby, stocky, and tough, the cold-chisel is designed to be driven with a hefty hammer. Using it, you can cut openings in metal, lop bolts in half, or sheer off immoveable nuts. Cold-chisels vary from ¼ to 1 inch wide.

Files and Rasp

These come in too many variations to list; they vary in shape (flat, half-round, round, square, triangular, etc.), length, and by the size of teeth. Going from coarse to smooth, the range is: bastard, second-cut, smooth-cut. For general home use, buy either second-cut or smooth-cut teeth in 12-inch length.

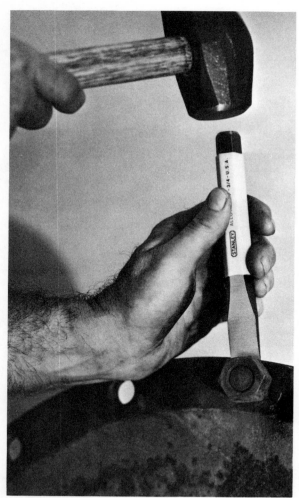
Cold-chisel

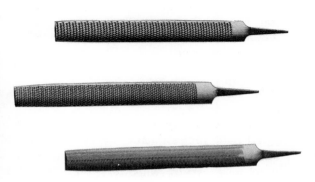
Files and rasp

Rasp teeth are very coarse and are intended for use on wood. With them, you can do a nice job of shaping or curving surfaces.

Knives

Pocketknife

Get a good, strong, well-built pocketknife or carving-blade knife; it has dozens of uses, from cutting string to carving joints in wood. Keep the blade sharp and keep the tool within easy reach. Don't be conned into buying one of those 82-use tools with a multitude of blades that open out to give you everything from a crosscut saw to a pair of cuticle scissors.

Carpenter's Knife

Sometimes known as a mason's knife, this exceedingly tough tool has a wedge-shaped, thick blade that can cut through almost anything you're strong enough to use it for — from tough canvas to homasote. The handle is thick, shaped just right for a firm grip, and several blades are stored in it.

Curved-blade Knife

A similar type has a curved blade, especially suited for cutting linoleum or carpeting. Usually it comes with its own handle but its separate curved blades also fit the carpenter's knife handle.

Ripping Bar

A rugged tool with a spike-puller and prying device at one end, and flattened and sometimes sharpened to chisel fineness at the other end, the ripping bar is used for prying between boards. The weekend carpenter usually finds the gooseneck bar more necessary than professionals do, possibly because it provides greater leverage.

Drills

Rotary Hand-drill

Although many home-carpenters drill small holes with a hand electric-drill, the manual device will do the job if you don't expect to drill more than a few holes or to work with hard metal.

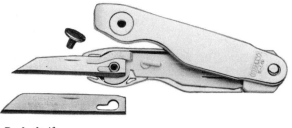
Pocketknife

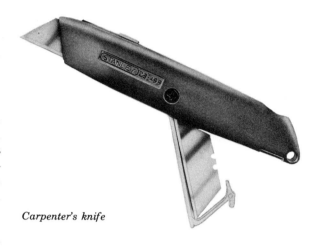
Carpenter's knife

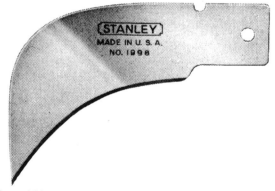
Curved-blade

Ripping-bar

Rotary hand-drill

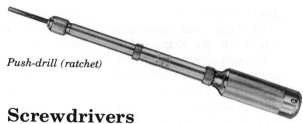

Push-drill (ratchet)

Push-drill (Ratchet Type)

You may prefer the one-handed action of the push-drill to the rotary type. Intended for light duty only, it often comes with its own assortment of drill-points contained in the handle. Fit one into the chuck, and you can drill holes by merely pushing on the tool. (See Chapter 10, How to Use Hand-tools.) A built-in rotary action turns the drill and a built-in spring releases it to starting position as soon as you withdraw the drill.

Bit-brace

You'll definitely need a bit-brace for boring large holes in wood. Smaller holes (½ inch and under) are bored with a push-drill or rotary drill. (If you intend to do a lot of drilling, see the section on electric-drills in Chapter 5, Power-tools.) Buy a brace with a ball-bearing mounted handle. It makes turning easier.

Augur-bits for a brace are made in sizes starting at ¼ inch and going up to about 1 inch. For anything larger than this, you'll find an expansion bit much handier. (See Chapter 10, How to Use Hand-tools.)

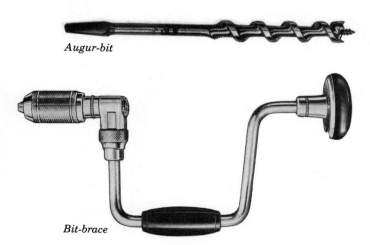

Augur-bit

Bit-brace

Screwdrivers

Standard and Phillips

There are two main types of screwdrivers: Standard *slotted* screwdrivers are the more common. However, there's a type of screw that has a cross-shaped slot in it called a Phillips head, for which you need a *Phillips* screwdriver. Both of these, slotted and Phillips, come in several different sizes, which means that you should acquire a number of screwdrivers. Buying sets seems the most sensible thing to do. A No. 1 size slotted screwdriver has a blade that is ⅛ inch wide at the tip. A No. 2 is ¼ inch wide; No. 3 is ⁵/₁₆ inch wide; No. 4 is ⅜ inch wide. Phillips screwdrivers come in a similar assortment; medium and small sizes will probably handle any job you need to tackle.

Push Screwdriver

Like the push-drill, there is a push screwdriver. Some push screwdrivers have several screwdriver heads, including Phillips, in a handle compartment. The bits fit into a chuck in the handle. (See Chapter 10, How to Use Hand-tools.) You may want this tool as an alternate to the standard and Phillips.

Counter-sink for Screws

Buy a counter-sink in several sizes for use with a screwdriver or with the hand-drill. This tool reams out a cone-shaped hole that will accept the head of a screw slightly below the top surface of the wood, so that it can be covered with wood-filler.

Pliers

Slipjoint Pliers

After the hammer, probably the most common household tool is one known as slipjoint pliers. These pliers have a joint that allows the jaws to be adjusted to two positions.

Lineman's Pliers

The next most used pliers have a metal snipper on the side, and are known as lineman's sidecutting pliers because most telephone repairmen couldn't do without them.

For these two tools, look for the words "drop forged" somewhere on the metal. This is a sign of quality, indicating that there will be no sloppy ridges of excess metal from poor casting.

(For more on the variety of pliers, snippers, wrenches, and their relatives, see Chapter 10, How to Use Hand-tools.)

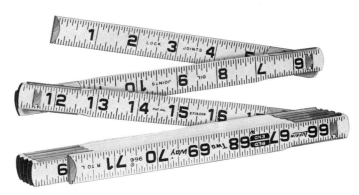

Zig-zag rule

Adjustable Wrench

For some reason, many people think of the adjustable wrench as the monkey-wrench. It is a smooth-jawed wrench that will adjust via a thumb-wheel, so that you can tighten square nuts, hex nuts, etc., with it.

Zig-zag Rule

This is the familiar wooden ruler that extends 6 feet. While metric calibrations are certainly coming in the near future, you're still better off now buying a ruler that is marked in inches and common fractions. For a bit of additional money, you can buy one called a fold-ing ruler, made with a brass extension slide at one end for taking measurements inside a small hole or crack. (See Chapter 10.)

Squares

Squares are not all the same. Many amateurs get along with the try square only, until they run into larger carpentry jobs.

Try Square

This one you'll need from the beginning just to square things up. You may want other squares, depending on the work you undertake.

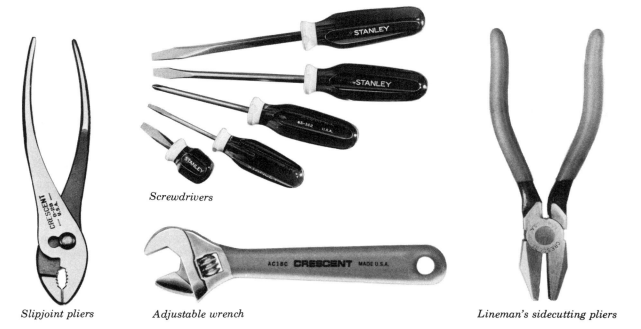

Slipjoint pliers   *Adjustable wrench*   *Screwdrivers*   *Lineman's sidecutting pliers*

Try-square

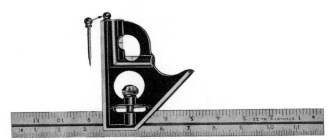

Combination square

Combination Square

This handy tool, usually no more than 12 inches long, is an alternate for the try square in checking a piece of wood for square surfaces. Mounted with a sliding steel ruler, it will also act as a level and indicate either 90-degree or 45-degree angles.

Level, Torpedo

This one is the little 6-inch household gadget you use to make sure your board ceiling is horizontal, vertical, or at 45 degrees. Don't confuse it with the carpenter's or household level, which is much longer and is used for major construction.

Hand Abrasives, Sandpaper

In the home build-it and fix-it field, the word *"abrasive"* generally means one thing — sandpaper. Actually, the field has expanded tremendously. "Coated abrasives" take in a host of materials, including silicone carbides, aluminum oxide, garnet flint, and emery, for cutting and smoothing surfaces. The material they are applied to can range from paper to cloth to metal mesh. (For types and variety of use, see Chapter 10, How to Use Hand-tools.)

Torpedo level

4
Second-stage Hand-tools

Once you have your basic tools, there's a wide assortment of additional tools that you may want to add to your collection as you find a need for them. Among hundreds, these would prove the most useful aid. For bigger construction jobs such as walls and decks, some are essential.

Hammers
When heavier hammers are required, the carpenter may need to use a ripping hammer (see Chapter 3) or a brick or masonry hammer. When ripping out walls (see Chapter 9), you will need either or both of these: the ripping hammer for plaster and the masonry hammer for brick, masonry, or concrete block walls.

Stapler
For many jobs, using a stapler is far speedier than hammering nails, but such heavy work as fastening hardware wire to wood will require a heavy-duty type of stapler, some of which are available electrically powered.

Mini Hacksaw
Because it has a rather bulky frame, a standard hacksaw cannot be used in a confined space. This tool consists of a small hand-grip attached to one end of the hacksaw blade, with the other end unsupported. Because the blade is not supported, you have to work more carefully, but can get the job done.

Surforming Shaver
An offshoot of the plane, this comparatively new type of tool does many of the same jobs. The narrow cutting surface has hundreds of tiny blades, and looks like the old-time nutmeg grater.

There are different models for different purposes. (See Chapter 10, How to Use Hand-tools.)

Tinsnips
The standard inexpensive variety of tinsnips looks like a jumbo pair of scissors and works much the same way, except that the material it cuts is sheet metal for such things as roof flashings.

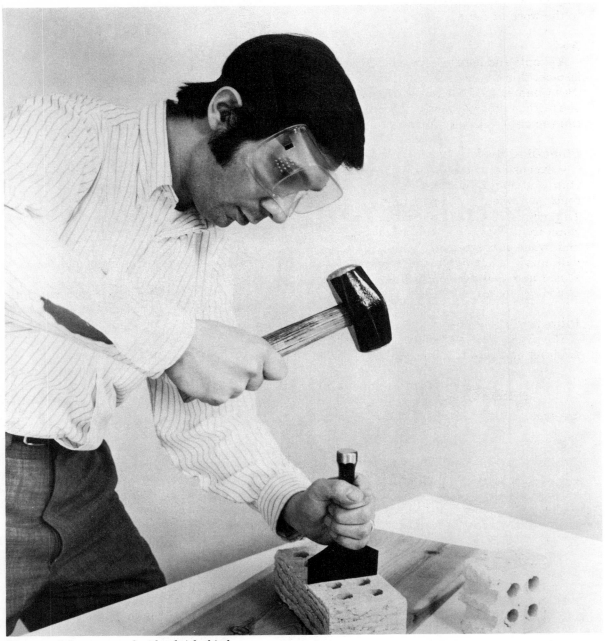

Heavy mash hammer used with a brick chisel

Airplane Shears

More costly than tinsnips, airplane shears operate with compound leverage, so you can slice through relatively heavy sheet metal with far less effort.

Multi-purpose Cutting Tool

In the jargon of the home-repair field, most craftsmen call this a "nibbler." It is sold with interchangeable cutting blades, each one designed for a specific range of materials. The only know-how required is to match the cutters to the work at hand.

Awl

A simple and inexpensive tool shaped like an icepick, this can be handy for all sorts of jobs. (See Chapter 10, How to Use Hand-tools.) Buy one with a sturdy plastic handle so that you can tap on it with a hammer.

Chalk-line Reel

Inexpensive, the chalk-line reel consists of sturdy string that rolls up inside a metal container when you turn a crank on the side. The gadget has a compartment for powdered chalk that coats the string as you draw it out, and, when it is stretched taut and snapped, it will mark a straight line. (See Chapter 8, Floors and Ceilings, and Chapter 10, How to Use Hand-tools.)

Plumb-bob and Line

The plumb-line is a string with a bob-weight at either end used to gauge a perpendicular for

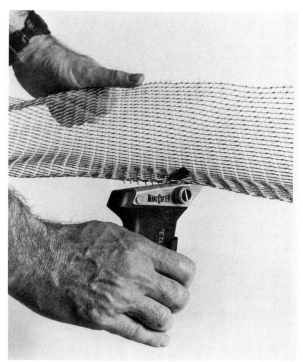

Multi-purpose cutting-tool, or "nibbler"

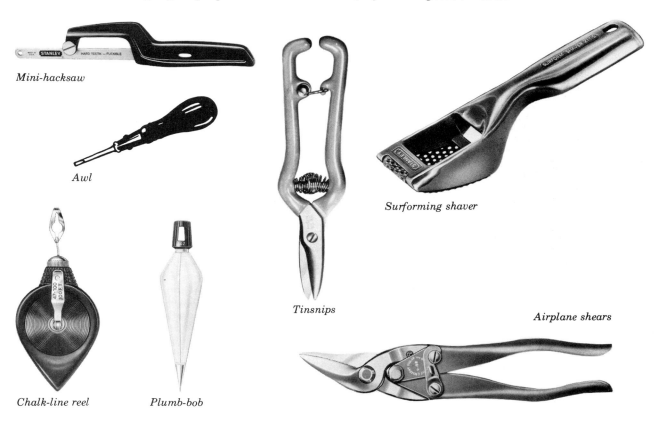

Mini-hacksaw

Awl

Tinsnips

Surforming shaver

Airplane shears

Chalk-line reel

Plumb-bob

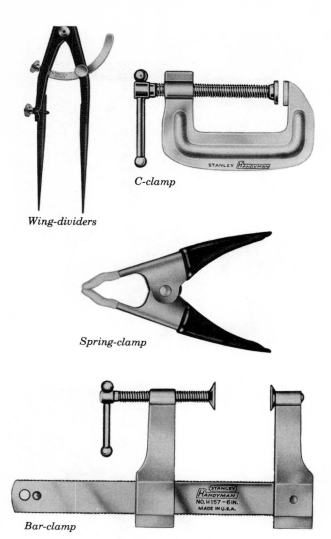

Wing-dividers

C-clamp

Spring-clamp

Bar-clamp

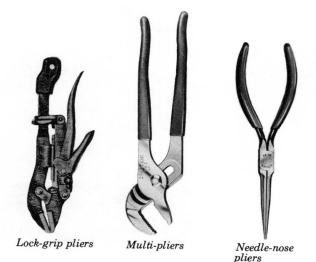

Lock-grip pliers   Multi-pliers   Needle-nose pliers

a wall or the level of a floor or a deck or ground. (See Chapter 6, Finishing Interior Walls, Kitchens, Baths.)

Wing Dividers

These have numerous uses, but for carpentry, there is no use more important than marking uneven wallboard to cut to fit. (See Chapter 6, Finishing Interior Walls, Kitchens, Baths.)

Clamps

Included in the category of clamps is a variety of specialized tools that differ in appearance and application. However, the purpose is the same: to hold things together. Most often you'll use them to keep wood sections in position while the glue that joins them sets and dries.

The adjustable "C" clamp is the most common variety. *Spring clamps* will do quite well for smaller jobs where heavy pressure isn't needed.

The pressure of a *bar clamp* is required for clamping action across a long span.

Wooden *hand-screw clamps* for cabinet-work adjust and contort to fit almost any job.

For special purposes, there are special clamps, such as a *band or web clamp* that applies the pressure to a canvas band. This tool is especially handy for such jobs as gluing the rungs into all four legs of a chair at one time.

Lock-grip Pliers

The mechanism of this tool is a sort of multi-adjustable pliers with one additional feature: the jaws can be set so that, when you squeeze the handles, they will grip and lock into position. As a result of this leverage, you can exert far more gripping force than with standard pliers. Also, once you have squeezed the handles together, these pliers will lock in that position until released by a pressure mechanism.

Multi-pliers

Many mechanics refer to these as water-pump pliers. The jaws are set at a wide angle with a long slipjoint and they open considerably wider than standard pliers.

Needle-nose Pliers

While not so common as other pliers, needle-nose pliers perform many delicate tasks, such as pulling a fine nail-head out of a piece of fine carpentry. Not necessary, but useful.

Pipe Wrench

The jaws of the pipe wrench are both adjustable and heavily serrated. In addition, the handle is long and the overall construction quite rugged. This hefty tool is designed to grasp a length of pipe so that you can either thread or unthread it.

Screw and Nut Starters

There will be times when it is impossible to get your hand into place to position a screw so that you can drive it home. The ingenious screw starter can save the day. It's designed to hold the screw on the end magnetically so that you can screw the first few threads into place. A similar tool works well for nuts that have to be screwed into out-of-the-way bolts.

Nut-Drivers and Wrenches

In the same way you use your car wrench to change a tire by screwing the nuts onto the wheel bolts, there are socket-type nut-drivers for screwing nuts onto fixed bolts that are increasingly popular among laymen. They come in sets of different sizes.

You can still get, or will receive, open-end and box wrenches with some tools, such as power chain-saws and grass-cutters.

Flexible Steel Tape

Although made in ranges from 6 feet to 16, the most popular size of flexible steel tape for all-around use is 10 feet long. As with the folding rule, buy one that is marked in inches and common fractions.

Long Non-metallic Measuring Tape

This does the measuring job over a great distance. It is available in lengths of 25, 50, 100 feet, and even more. Since the spring-action that is used on the steel tape is impractical in this length, there should be a crank handle on the side for this purpose.

Pipe wrench (Stillson)

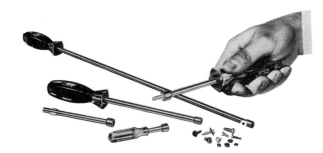

Magnetic screw and nut starters

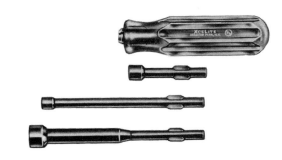

Socket-type nut-driver, handle and attachments

Box wrenches and open-end wrenches

Flexible steel tape

Long non-metallic measuring tape

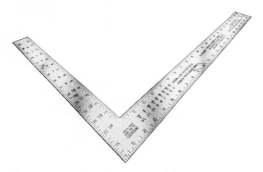

Carpenter's square (homeowner's)

Carpenter's Square (Homeowner's)

In measuring and squaring sizeable jobs, it's almost impossible to manage without a large, 24x16-inch steel framing-square. You will find a wealth of information on the blades. In addition to the standard scale of inches, they contain data to make many other estimates. You will need one if you are going to put up roof-framing or construct a wall or stairs. (See Chapter 7, Putting up Partition Walls and Their Doors.)

Carpenter's Level

This tool contains two or more liquid bubble tubes mounted in a long frame, giving a true indication of vertical, level, or 45-degree positions. For durability as well as reliability, buy a level with a body made of aluminum. Besides being lighter, it will not warp or rust. Generally, for major carpentry, you should select a level that is 18 to 48 inches long, instead of the short torpedo level.

Line Level

A very lightweight line level is hung on the plumb-line in leveling the line. (See page 104.)

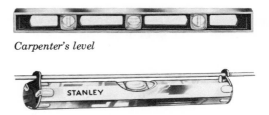

Carpenter's level

Line level

5
Power-tools

After you have tackled a few home-building or repair projects, you will probably become either lazy or ambitious. Many projects can be accomplished with even one or two of the power-tools displayed on the shelves of your local hardware store at far less cost than they would run if you hired a professional carpenter or bought what you needed ready-built. These tools can save you an enormous amount of time and can accomplish the job far more easily than would be possible without them. However, as with hand-tools, the caution for buying power-tools is "slowly and carefully." Power-up for the job with as little expense as possible, and remember that you may need a cautious helper. Power-tools must be understood by the person using them.

Portable-electric Hand-saw

Selecting a Power-saw
The hand electric saw is the workhorse of the amateur, though the professional carpenter might give no particular thought to it. Although exact estimates are hard to come by, it's a safe guess that you can do about a hundred times the amount of work with a power-saw as you could accomplish in the same time with a battery of hand-saws.

The available assortment lined up on your dealer's shelves may be bewildering: each tool may have more than ten types of blades in various sizes for various purposes. However, there are a few guidelines that will help you select the proper tool for your use. Make certain, for example, that the saw can cut through a 2x4 at a 45-degree angle as well as a 90-degree angle. This means that the diameter of the blade should be a bit more than 7 inches. Because of this ratio, there are a great many saws on the market with blades 7⅛ or 7¼ inches in diameter.

The tool should have a depth adjustment. This feature is needed for making shallow cuts through thin stock, and it is useful when you don't want to saw entirely through a piece of lumber.

Check, too, for an angle adjustment so that you can cut miters and bevels. For ease in ripping a board to specific widths, a ripping-gauge is handy.

Circular saw with blade guard and angle adjustment

Virtually all hand electric-saws have an automatic blade-guard attached to a spring mechanism. As you cut into a board, the blade-guard retracts. As you finish the cut on the other side, the blade-guard swings back to cover the exposed section of the saw-blade. It's an essential safety feature.

Beyond these specific functions (which almost all hand power-saws have), there are a few intangibles that should guide your selection. For example, make sure the tool feels comfortable in your hand. Since it can weigh from 8 to 18 pounds, you need sufficient heft in your good right arm for as long a period as you will be operating it. Make sure that the handle is comfortable, and that the starting switch is close to your trigger-finger and that it operates easily. An additional feature (although not absolutely necessary) is a second knob handle, which is usually positioned some distance from the main supporting handle. This can aid in guiding the tool or in supporting it.

Using the Saw

It is preferable to wear goggles with side shields. Adjust the depth of cut so that the saw-blade protrudes no more than ¼ inch through the work. Practice maintaining an even, forward stroke. Any sort of a zig-zag action will tend to bind the saw in the cut.

Make absolutely certain that the work you are cutting is firmly supported. The motor is powerful; if the work should twist, bind, or jam against the saw-blade, one of two things can happen. Either the tool itself can kick up and out of the work, or the board can be sent skittering. Both are risky.

Start the saw-blade turning before you touch it to the work, and guide the tool carefully and easily along the cutting-line you have made. Most hand electric-saws have a notched guide intended to follow this line. If you cradle the marked line with the guide, you are well on your way to a straight cut.

Needless to say, the cord to the tool should be kept well out of the way. It's more than embarrassing to zip right through it with one powerful stroke.

Maintain even pressure throughout the entire cut. This is especially important for the end of the line. Make certain you don't allow the blade to drop or tip just as you finish. After sawing as far as you want to go, allow the blade to come to a complete stop and lift the saw clear of the work so that the spring-loaded guard snaps shut around the cutting-edges.

As a general safety precaution, unplug the tool before you change the tilt, depth of cut, or any other adjustment. Disconnect the saw immediately after finishing a job; children or

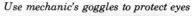

Use mechanic's goggles to protect eyes

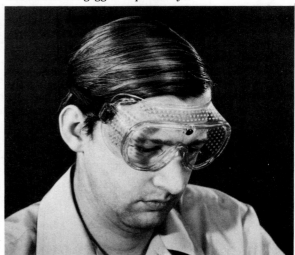

Blade Diameter

6" to 8"	Carbide-Tipped	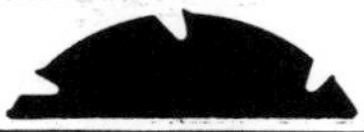	6½" to 8"	Combination	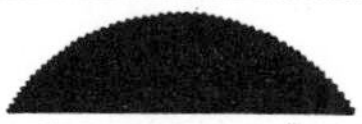
6" to 8¼"	Crosscut		6½" to 8"	Rip	
6" to 8¼"	Rip	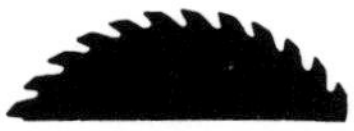	6½" to 8"	Crosscut	
6" to 8¼"	Chisel Tooth		6½" to 8"	Plywood	
6" to 8¼"	Hollow Ground		6½" to 8"	Flooring	

Portable circular-saw accessories for two different types of Rockwell circular saws

Blade Diameter	Recommend Use	
5⅞"	Plywood cutting	
6"	Sizing hardwood flooring	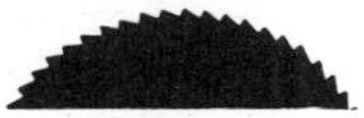
6⅜"	Cutting light gauge metals; Transite and Fiberglas	
6½"	Plywood cutting	
6¾"	General ripping and crosscutting	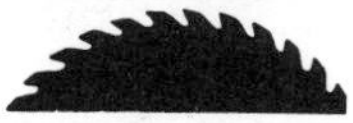
7"	Plywood cutting	
7¼"	Plywood cutting	
7½"	General ripping and crosscutting	
8"	Plywood cutting and finishing of woods. All-purpose for difficult sawing jobs.	 
9"	Cutting hardwoods and plastic; lightweight aluminum extrusions and soft non-ferrous metals (with lubricant)	

Portable circular-saw accessories

animals, attracted by the noise, may get at the tool as soon as your back is turned.

When you replace the blade, make certain it's positioned so that it will turn in the right direction. If you have any doubts, look for an arrow printed on the blade.

Many different types of blades are available for these tools. For general all-around use, there's a combination blade that combines crosscut and rip. It will do a good job on most types of lumber, and works reasonably well on plywood, too. For cutting large amounts of plywood or for cabinet-work, crosscut blades will give smoother cuts.

As with a hand-saw, rip-blades do a much better and faster job if you have to cut boards into long strips working with the grain. For the smoothest cut of all, try a hollow-ground blade. This is a strange-looking affair combining groups of saw-teeth separated by deep notches. In spite of its appearance, it will do the job at a satisfying rate and leave a surface that needs little or no sanding.

Don't attempt to sharpen the blades yourself.

Cordless electric-drill

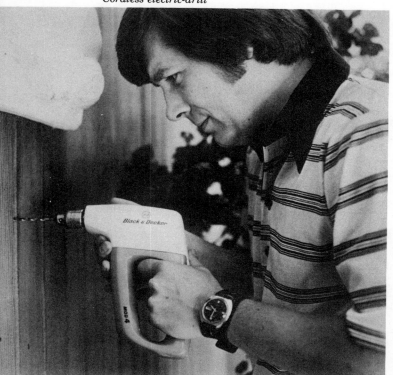

Keep an extra blade on hand so that you can keep working while a dull blade is being professionally sharpened.

After a while, you will get the knack of some special cuts that are delightfully easy with a hand electric-saw. A good example of this is a pocket-cut. As the name implies, this is a section or pocket that is cut out of the center of a board or plywood sheet. To complete this maneuver, have the saw running and the blade-guard retracted as you slowly tilt the saw forward and lower the blade into the wood. You'll have to finish up the corners of the square with a hand-saw, but this final bit of work requires minimum effort.

Electric-Drill

Among carpenters it's known as a "palmful of power," and that just about describes it. At a touch of the trigger, you've got pure, unadulterated moxie ready for all the tough jobs at hand. Actual power can range from $1/5$ horsepower to as much as $1½$ horsepower. With this force, you can drill metal, wood, plastic, and even concrete.

Selecting a Drill

The size of the chuck determines the designation of the drill, and this depends on the largest-size bit that will go into the gadget. For example, a ¼-inch electric-drill will turn a bit up to ¼ inch in size. There are similar versions in ⅜, ½, and even ¾ inch, although these are not usually necessary for the average home workshop. You will find quite a bit of variation in power as well as speed. The range of power in a ¼-inch drill is generally from $1/5$ to $1/4$ horsepower.

Hooked up to an increasingly versatile assortment of accessories, the drill with different-size chucks can double as a shaver grindstone, power rasp, sander, polisher, socket wrench, and even screwdriver (slotted or Phillips).

As far as turning speed is concerned, the smaller sizes generally whirl at a faster rate. For example, a ¼-inch drill may turn as fast as 2000 rpm, while a ½-inch drill may rotate at only 600 rpm. Since the larger drills use larger

How to select the right drill for the task – note versatility of variable-speed drill

Use	Wood	Metal	Sand	Grind	Polish	Masonry	Glass	Drive Screws	Remove Screws
Single-speed									
Variable-speed / **Adjustable Variable-speed**									
Adjustable Variable-speed reversing									

How to select the right chuck-size

1/4 inch	Drilling capacity: ¼-inch in steel, ½-inch in wood. Recommended for small-hole drilling in softer materials. 2300 rpm ideal for polishing, grinding, and sanding.
3/8 inch	Larger capacity permits ⅜-inch holes in steel, ¾-inch in wood. Provides more power and greater torque at low rpm and is well suited to drilling harder metals, concrete, and glass.
1/2 inch	Drills up to 1-inch in wood, ½-inch in steel, concrete, and cast iron. Recommended for frequent and prolonged drilling in hard materials.

drill-bits, these slow speeds provide the greater power that is needed to turn them.

There may be other variations, though not all of them are apparent on the surface. For example, most drills come in regular and heavy-duty models. The difference usually involves such things as ball- or roller-bearings for the jumbo version and oiled bronze-bearings for light-duty use. On a strictly short-term basis, there really isn't any reason for you to invest in a heavy-duty drill for normal household tasks. However, this is one area where normal prudence may be bent slightly if your finances can take the strain. A heavy-duty drill with a full complement of roller- or

ball-bearings will last far longer, will maintain precision over a much longer period, and will have a better feel in use. Admittedly, this is a subjective point, but try it out and determine for yourself.

One additional feature that's showing up on many electric-drills these days is a variable speed-control. The trigger-switch, instead of merely turning the tool on and off, actually adjusts the speed at which the chuck turns. Barely ease back on the trigger, and the chuck will turn over so slowly that you can actually count the revolutions. Pull it all the way back, and you've got top speed. In between these two speeds are infinite variations. This feature

Electric-drill guide

Guide assures straight drilling

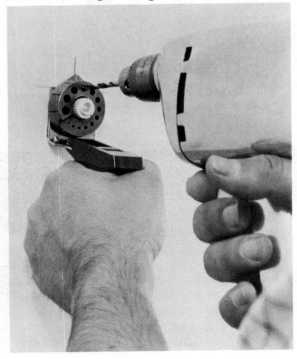

allows you to select the best speed for each task. For example, if you are driving screws with the drill, a slow speed is preferable.

Some drills are also equipped with a reverse switch. This feature gives you the option of backing a bit out of a deep hole in the wood and allows you to remove screws.

Bits

Be sure to use the special drill-bits that are made for power applications. They are manufactured from a tougher metal that will stand up to the heat, speed, and stress. In addition to the standard twist-drill configuration, you will also find bits of the augur type. They look similar to the variety used with a bit-brace except that there is no screw-tip at the end.

Electric-drills can also utilize what's known as a "spade-bit." This has no spiral shank at all. The cutting-end is flat. At first glance, it would not seem to be a very efficient cutting tool, but a test-run will give you a great deal more respect for this handy gadget.

For precision drilling, there's a special guide to make you drill straight. Some amateurs may need it for all this drill-work.

If you're going to drill holes in brick or masonry, you'll have to invest in special carbide-tip drills meant specifically for this job. Work with a slow speed and lots of pressure. There's one other item called an "oversized drill-bit" that you should know about. This has a shank of a smaller diameter, so you can fit a ½-inch bit into the chuck of a ¼-inch drill. A very handy idea indeed, but you can overload the power beyond the manufacturer's specifications if you drill with a heavy touch. If you have much of this work to do, better plan on investing in a larger-size electric-drill. In any case, wear rubber gloves and goggles.

Sanders and Polishers

Hand-sanding can be one of the most laborious tasks for the amateur. There's plenty of recreational work to carpentry without laboring unnecessarily.

Belt-sander

The belt-sander is a handy little device taking little strength, and a youngster in the family may enjoy sanding down a wood-paneled wall for refinishing, or the wooden coffee table that should have been refinished a decade ago. Some companies offer a belt-sander that also acts as a most effective *polisher*.

Disc-sander

A disc-sander in the hands of an amateur is likely to leave circular marks, though it does a fine job of polishing. Both belt- and disc-sanders are good paint-removers. And your hand electric-drill may be equipped to do both these jobs in rotary motion, but of course not in straight belt-sanding.

Floor-sanding is a different matter. If you rent a floor-sander, you'll need the hand electric-sander to clean up the corners, window-sills, and other small surfaces.

(For abrasives and sandpapers, see Chapter 10, How to Use Hand-tools.)

Electric Jigsaw

These jigsaws are a versatile group not to be thought of as confined to making puzzles, although they can do this. As you can see from the variety of attachable blades, they can cut everything from a 6x6-inch rafter to a plastic daisy. Unless you are a master craftsman, you may have little use for this specialty tool.

Electric-Chisel or Router

Unless the amateur becomes carried away with making furniture with intricate joints, or with creating original moldings not to be found at the lumberyard or hardware store, the hand electric-chisels and routers are not for him. But, since many terms for cuts and joints have become familiar to the layman, a brief rundown appears on page 41.

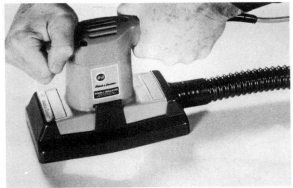
Belt-sander

Sander with polisher attachment

Jigsaw

Disc sander

Jigsaw Blades and Their Uses

Jigsaw blades	Blade Type	Description of Blade and Use	Type of Cut	Speed of Cut
	Flush cutting	Hard or soft wood over ¼" thick.	Rough	Fast
	Plaster cutting	V-tooth design provides constant abrading action effective in cutting plaster, masonry, and high-density plastics.	Rough	Fast
	Double cutting	Most wood and fiber materials. Tooth design allows for cutting in both directions with equal speed.	Rough	Fast
	Skip tooth	Cuts most plastics and plywoods.	Rough	Fast
	Double cutting	Cuts most wood and fiber materials. Tooth design allows for cutting in both directions with equal speed and quality of cut.	Medium	Medium
	Wood cutting coarse	Cuts soft woods ¾" and thicker.	Rough	Fastest
	Wood cutting fine	Cuts soft woods under ¾" thick.	Medium	Medium
	Wood cutting hollow ground	Hard woods under ¾" thick.	Smooth	Medium
	Metal cutting	For cutting ferrous (iron) metals ¼" to ⅜" thick and nonferrous (aluminum, copper, etc.) ⅛" to ¼".	Medium	Medium
	Metal cutting	For ferrous metals ⅛" to ¼" thick and nonferrous metals ¹⁄₁₆" to ⅛".	Smooth	Medium
	Metal cutting	For ferrous metals ¹⁄₁₆" to ³⁄₁₆" thick.	Fine	Slow
	Metal cutting	For ferrous metals hard ¹⁄₆₄" to ³⁄₃₂" thick.	Very fine	Slow
	Hollow ground	For cutting plywoods ½" to ¾" thick. For fine finish work. Hollow ground for absolutely smooth finish on all wood products.	Extremely fine	Medium
	Hollow ground	For cutting plywood and finish materials ¾" and thicker where fine finish is desirable.	Smooth	Medium
	Hollow ground	For cutting soft woods up to 2" thick where fine finish is desirable. Thicker blade provides less flexing when cutting 1" to 2" thick. Not recommended for scroll-type cutting.	Smooth	Medium
	Hollow ground	For cutting plywood up to 1" thick.	Fine	Medium
	Hollow ground	For cutting plywood ¾" thick and under.	Smooth	Medium-Fast
	Hollow ground	For plywood ¼" to 1" thick.	Medium	Fast
	Knife blade	For cutting leather, rubber, composition tile, cardboard, etc.	Smooth	Fast
	Fleam ground	For cutting green or wet woods ¼" to 1½" thick. Fleam ground provides shredding type cutting action effective in sawing hard, green or wet materials.	Smooth	Medium
	Fleam ground	For cutting green or wet woods ⅜" to 2½" thick.	Coarse	Fast
	Scroll	For cutting wood, plastic and plywood ¼" to 1" thick. Set teeth and thin construction allows this blade to make intricate cuts and circles with radii as small as ⅛".	Smooth	Medium
	Wood cutting coarse	Cuts most plastics and wood up to 4" thick. Special tooth design with extra large gullets provides extra chip clearance for fast cutting in thicker materials.	Rough	Fast
	Wood cutting medium	Makes fairly smooth cuts in wood up to 4" thick. Extra thick back provides greater resistance to breaking during intricate scroll-type cutting.	Medium	Medium

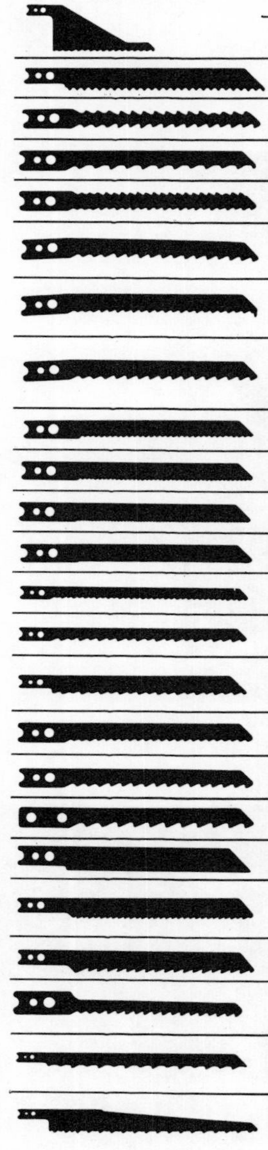

Hand electric-chisel

Tenon fits into mortise carved by chisel or router

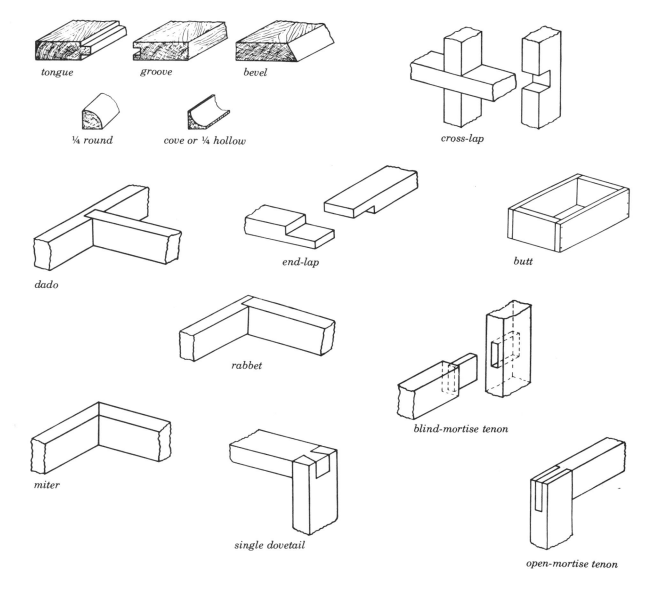

tongue   *groove*   *bevel*

¼ round   *cove or ¼ hollow*

cross-lap

dado

end-lap

butt

rabbet

blind-mortise tenon

miter

single dovetail

open-mortise tenon

Two types of three-pronged plugs

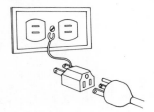

Two-prong adapter plug with metal clip, which fits under screw of outlet plate to ground current

Safety

Goggles and rubber gloves have already been mentioned, but there are other safety precautions. You should make quite sure the electric-tool you select has one of two electrical safety precautions built into it.

Three-wire Grounding

Because there is always a shock hazard when using any electrical appliance, be sure every electric-tool is equipped with a three-wire grounding cord. It's easy to spot. The male plug at the end of the cord will have two flat prongs plus a round pin that's slightly longer. Such a cord can only be used in a three-wire outlet or with a special adapter plug.

Double-insulated

Do not panic if the tool you want to buy comes with literature that makes a whole to-do about safety features but is equipped with a two-pronged plug minus the round grounding-pin. Keep reading to find out if the electric-tool is a type known as double-insulated. In these, the outer shell as well as the chuck (in other words, the parts that you can actually come into contact with) are completely insulated from the wiring and electrical mechanism. But if not marked "double-insulated," the cord *must* have a three-wire cord, as described above, and you

should wear rubber, not plastic, gloves so the current cannot be transmitted to your body. This can save you the possibility of severe shock, if not worse.

Extension-cords

Many electric-tools come with a heavy-duty extension-cord that plugs right into the instrument, replacing the regular 6-foot cord with a 25-footer that's either the two- or three-wire variety. If yours has a three-wire cord, don't bypass it by using a two-wire extension-cord. Buy a three-wire extension made specifically for this. Also make certain it is a heavy-duty extension cord. The wires should be at least as heavy as those in the tool-cord itself. If you need an extension that's more than 10 or 15 feet long, the wires should be even heavier to avoid power loss.

Three-wire cords come with an adapter so that you can plug them into a regular wall-socket safely. One end of the adapter will accept the two prongs and the round connector. The other end contains only two prongs but it has a short length of wire with a little clip sticking out of it. That clip is meant to be screwed under one of the metal screws holding the electric switch-plate to the wall. *This step is very important. It completes the ground connection.* The three-wire system on your electric-tool is absolutely worthless unless you follow this important procedure. If you neglect to ground the power, you may receive an electric charge which you could avoid with the switch-plate clip or rubber gloves or dry rubber soles. Without the three-wire heavy-duty cord and the grounding-wire of an extension attached to the receptacle plate, you could get a nasty electrical surprise, especially in wet weather, because water conducts electricity. The same is true of touching an active electrical device while standing in the water of a bathtub. You may not be electrocuted but you will receive electricity until the electrical connection through your body is broken. And with an electric-saw, it is sometimes hard to let go, to break the electrical circuit.

6
Finishing Interior Walls, Kitchens, Baths

Plywood paneling is becoming increasingly popular these days. But don't think it's just the fir plywood with all that dark squiggly grain. For paneling walls, plywood now comes with a wide variety of exotic veneers. You can have walnut, cherry, maple, birch, even things like wormy chestnut or soft mellow woods like butternut. The variety is truly amazing. For a sampling, check through the stock at your local lumberyard or building-supply company.

Pre-finished Panels

Be sure to buy pre-finished panels, however. Although you can save money by buying veneer in its natural state to make your own panels, the labor of finishing isn't worth the economy.

Since the standard panel is 4x8 feet and the studs are 16 inches apart in their centers, you can easily glue or nail each panel to the center of a joist. But in older houses, this is not always the case. If the studs in the wall are irregularly spaced, or if you're going to use a material that's supplied in narrow vertical strips, your best bet is to put up furring strips. (See illustrations in Chapter 7 showing furring strips.) These are simply long strips of wood 3 or 4 inches wide and about ¾ inch thick. They are nailed horizontally across the stud wall to act as a nailing surface for the vertical wall-paneling.

Fasten one furring strip to the top and one to the bottom of the stud wall. Attach another one in the center, and space the remaining two equally between. No need to get fancy about applying them. Just drive a nail through one end and level the other by eye. It's good building practice to attach each furring strip to each stud using common nails.

Before you head for the lumberyard, spend a little time planning the job, whether it's an old house or a new one you are working on. You'll be sure to save some money this way.

Material Calculations

It's relatively simple to figure out the number of sheets you will need to panel a room. First multiply the height and width for each wall, then add together the areas of all four walls. Now multiply the height and width of each

Pine wall and matching cupboards

Redwood paneling

door- and window-opening, and add all these totals together. Subtract the door and window totals from the room area. This will give you the actual square-footage to be covered.

Decide upon the size of the panel that you will use, and multiply its length by its width. Divide this figure into the square-footage to be covered. The final tally will give you an indication of the number of panels you have to buy. Add about 10 percent for waste, as not every piece will fit perfectly.

While this system isn't ironclad, it will give you a fairly close approximation.

We have stated that the standard-size panel is 4x8 feet (the standard height of a ceiling in modern construction). They also come shorter and longer, but these sizes are generally not as readily available. Plan the way you will cut the sheets to cover the space below windows, above cabinets, etc. Try to utilize the odd segments that you'll be cutting out. If you can do the job with one less sheet of paneling, you will wind up with a handy saving.

After the panels have been delivered, store them in a heated room — preferably the room where they will be installed — for several days before you actually start work. This will give the wood time to shrink or swell to house temperature and will keep the panels from pulling apart at the joints or buckling later on.

Before you put up the first panel, take a few minutes to juggle the wood-sections around until you get a matching of the grain on the panels that appeals to you. Since wood is a natural material, there's bound to be some variation from panel to panel.

Incidentally, the panels are not heavy. The standard 4x8-foot size of ¼-inch thickness weighs only about 24 pounds. This means that you can heft it into place by yourself.

Installation

Start paneling in one corner of the room. Hang a plumb-bob (see Chapter 4) against the outer edge of this first panel and shift the plywood back and forth slightly until the edge of it lines up with the string of the plumb-bob.

It's an almost sure bet that the edge of the panel against the corner will now be pulled away at an angle. Unless you put up a new house with 2x4 studding with micrometer precision, there's bound to be some deviation. Even if you work carefully and still fail to spot any inaccuracies, they are bound to show up in operations like this. No problem really. The solution is simply to scribe and trim the plywood panel to fit the space exactly. Here's how to do that.

Set a pencil-compass so the space between the point and the pencil is a little more than the width of the largest gap between the board and the corner. Check to make certain that the other edge of the board is still perfectly aligned with the plumb-bob.

Run the compass pencil down the panel, with the point riding against the adjacent wall and the pencil making a continuous line on the panel. If you saw the panel off carefully along this pencil-line, the panel should now fit perfectly into the corner. At the same time, the other edge should still be absolutely vertical. This is an important step in paneling a room. Don't be discouraged. It's also one of the few operations that requires this much precision.

When you nail up your panels, No. 19 wire-brads ¾-inch-long are big enough to use. They make a smaller hole than a finishing-nail. After you have fastened up all the panels, sink the heads of the brads slightly below the surface. If necessary, you can fill the holes with tinted filler. (Some panels overlap, and the nails on the inner panel are covered.)

You may prefer to utilize a mastic or glue system of holding the panels to the studs. It does make a neater job without any nail-holes, which is an advantage if you are installing fancy prefinished paneling.

Fasten the second panel in place, butting the edges against the first one. To hide the joints, use the flat molding that is rounded at the edges. It is sold to match the paneling in the same lengths as the paneling. Some panels have special aluminum moldings covered with matching wood veneer. For a standard butt-joint between sheets, slip the molding over the edge of the panel and then nail it to the furring strips. Slide the next panel in on the other side of the molding, and continue. The same molding is manufactured in a different configuration for inside corners and ceiling molding. All of them conform to the ¼-inch panels and make a neat joint.

Mark the panel with a compass-pencil to cut to fit an uneven board, post, or chimney.

After glue-cementing the panel to furring-strips or studs, hold panel away from wall at the bottom with a block for 5 to 10 minutes until cement has set, then press back.

Needless to say, all electrical wiring is installed before the paneling is erected. In most states, electrical regulations and inspection are required.

Back-up clip

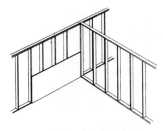

Horizontal wall-paneling. After all clips are installed, position drywall or paneling so that the end to be supported rests fully and squarely against the two tabs projecting from the clip. Nail material to studs so that the supported end "floats" against tabs.

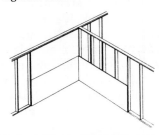

Wall-panel in back-up clips. After drywall or paneling has been positioned and nailed as outlined above, position wall-surfacing material on adjoining wall so that it covers the nailing tab of clip and fits firmly against the drywall or paneling already in place. Nail to studs.

Gluing Panels

In installing new panels, it is not necessary to tear out existing walls. New panels may be installed over existing or plaster walls so long as everything is in plumb, and so long as the new panels match closely enough at their joints to be covered by their matching moldings. Apply parallel rows of a cement intended for this purpose every few inches on the back of the panel and prop it on a thin block of wood on the floor. (The gap will be covered by the floorboard.) Press the cemented panel to the wall. Nail the panel at the top, but pull the bottom away, blocking it open for a few minutes — five to ten — until the cement has had time to set; then push it against the wall, and press the cement firmly by striking the panel with a block of wood wrapped in cloth to make sure it adheres. Then toenail the panel to the furring strips or studs.

For inside corners, the simplest system is to make a right-angle butt-joint, without molding. If you work carefully, this will give a simple handsome effect.

Don't worry too much about the areas where the plywood fits around electrical outlets, windows, and doors. The fit here does not have to be tight or precise. Later, when you apply trim, you will cover any imperfections.

Where a new wall or ceiling is installed on studs, metal connectors or back-up clips can be fastened to the studs or ceiling-plate and raf-

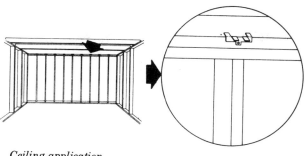

Ceiling application

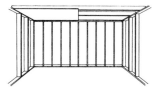

First ceiling-panel in place. Cut ceiling material for snug fit against tabs. Let end of material "hang" temporarily, if rigid.

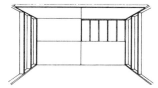

Ceiling and wall. Apply wall-surfacing material. When fitting and positioning top course of materials, be sure that there is a snug fit against the ceiling material so that it is firmly supported and pushed fully against the clip. Nail wall material.

The completed room. (See next chapter for the wall-building sequence which created this room.)

ters to hold plasterboard or panels in position. These clips hold the panels either vertically or horizontally and quickly build the new wall. When the clips are firmly nailed to the ceiling-plate, plasterboard or paneling can be equally firmly affixed to form the ceiling and be nailed to ceiling rafters. It will not be long before the new room has taken shape.

Finishing

When all the panels have been installed, you can turn your attention to the floorboards, the ceiling or crown moldings, and the windows and doors.

With plain floor-moldings that are rounded at the top, and with ceiling-moldings that are quarter-rounds or quarter-hollow (or cove) moldings, there's the matter of cutting to fit that you have with picture-moldings of this shape. But ceiling-moldings are not fitted together like picture-moldings; you have to fit them at outside corners, where there is a jut in the room, or at inside corners.

For coped or inside corner joints:

1. Cut moldings for the long sides of the room $1/16$ inch longer than the length of the ceiling. Use miter box to cut the ends square. Install the molding with a slight bow, and snap it into place, nailing it with brads or finishing-nails set in with a nail-set, to be filled in with wood-filler.

1. A miter box and a backsaw are used to square ends of the molding cut to fit the long side of the room.

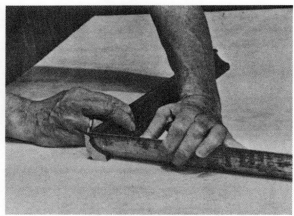

A rear-view showing how the coped piece of molding fits snugly against the molding cut with a square end.

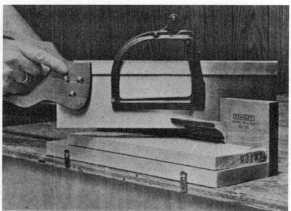

2. Hold the molding for short side of ceiling in the same position it will occupy when installed and make a 45-degree cut as shown.

Outside corner-moldings are simple 45-degree cuts made in the miter box.

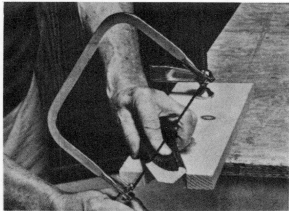

3. Use a coping saw to cut away the molding, following the edge of the miter-cut as a guide. Cut at slight backward angle.

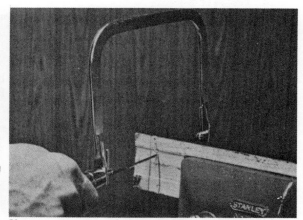

If paper pattern is used, secure molding in vise, tape front to prevent splintering, and use coping saw to make cut following pencil-mark.

2. The other sides must be cut with each end fitted to the shape of the molding already in place. To do this, cut a 45-degree angle in the end of the side molding, ceiling-side upward.

3. The 45-degree end is now cut with a coping saw (which is why it is called a coped joint) to fit the corner where the long molding is already in place. Cut the 45-degree corner with a coping saw tilted slightly inward, toward your left hand. This will give the necessary clearance when placing the second molding against the one in place. Any irregularities can be filled with wood-filler.

The same is done for floor-moldings, except that the 45-degree cut in the fitted molding is done with the floor-side downward.

The preceding is a coped joint, suitable only for an inside corner. For an outside corner joint, a mitered joint must be made. Both of the two joining moldings are cut in the miter box with a 45-degree cut, the ceiling-side of the moldings placed upward in the miter box.

If unsuccessful with either joint, make a paper cutout and use it to mark the necessary cut on the back of the molding.

In any case, before cutting molding, apply paper masking tape to the finished side of the molding, and mark the tape, then cut without fear of splintering the molding.

With floor-moldings, it is best to use screws rather than nails, so the moldings can be removed easily for wall-coverings that may be changed in the future, or to refit the molding to

Kitchen with ceiling and wall panels.

Substantial traditional redwood paneling gives a rich look for a bathroom ceiling, walls, and moisture-laden interior-garden walls.

great invention, doing away with laborious installations of tiling, with the necessity for repairing or grouting the tiles.

This fake tile paneling has not yet been developed to the attractiveness of real tile, so if you can afford tile and its installation (though you *can* do it yourself), you will have a far more handsome installation. There is, however, attractive and most satisfactory paneling that does not attempt to imitate expensive bathroom tiles, and you can install it yourself at a fraction of the cost of tile. But precision of cut and fit are not simple, although butt-joints and wall-corner and even ceiling waterproof moldings of matching materials are available.

Solid-wood Board Paneling

When buying solid-wood board paneling, calculate the material you will need and have

permit wall-to-wall carpeting to be fitted under it.

Kitchen and Bathroom Paneling

The procedure for kitchens and bathrooms is precisely the same, except that you will probably be working with walls already built. Furring the studs is essential, and it is more intricate than it is with other walls because you have to work around fixtures already installed. You will want to check the insulation inside the walls, and if it is not in good condition (mice will eat practically anything except fiberglass insulation), replace it.

Kitchen paneling can be much like that of other rooms, although it is important to remember in selecting the paneling that there's a lot more moisture and grease buildup in kitchens, and you will want to be able to wash the walls.

For bathrooms, there are special surfaces, such as formica-finished plywood, that are so moisture-proof that they can be used for lining showers and bathtubs. These surfaces are a

Intricate work with boards and plywood in combination for a spectacular picture window, beamed wooden ceiling, and window-seat with built-in cupboards. The skill of an architect and the craftsmanship of a cabinet-maker are needed for such an effect.

Unusual vertical strip-panels

Vertical panel boards should go up on furring strips. As with plywood, the first strip or panel is the most critical. Following the same scribing technique, mark the piece of wood so that it will fit flush into the corner of the wall. Trim it along the marked line, fit it snugly into place and flush-nail it at the very corner. Fasten the other side of the board to the furring strips with 2-inch-long floor-nails. Since you have trimmed the groove edge of the board to fit into the corner, the edge projecting out is the one with the tongue milled into it. Hammer the nails into the wood at the base of this tongue. Drive them in place at a 45-degree angle. Be very careful not to batter the wood. Hammer the last ¼-inch of the nail in using a nail-set. Cut the next board to proper length, slip it in place against the previous one, and then force the

it delivered several days before the job so that you can allow it to come up to room temperature. (Don't expect it to be as inexpensive as paneling!) Before you start the actual work, line up the sections of wood and arrange them so that you will have a pleasant flow of grain as well as an interesting variation in tone. Many people have a great affection for knotty pine. (Some homeowners may want a unique effect, such as the one shown in the illustration included here.)

Most solid-wood paneling is available in either uniform-width boards or random dimensions generally of 4, 6, and 8 inches. Most homeowners like to take advantage of the random widths, feeling that they make the finished job more attractive. Obviously, ¾-inch solid boards are more expensive than ¼-inch plywood paneling, but you may wish the richer, more traditional appearance.

Although you'll find quite a bit of variation, most solid-wood paneling comes in a standard ¾-inch thickness. It will probably be surfaced at the factory and might have the top surface (the one that will face out into the room) sanded smooth. In addition, the edges will probably be milled in a tongue-and-groove configuration.

This country lodge interior stresses vertical boards, timbers, a rugged platform, and ceiling with double beams. Furring strips were important in forming these walls, alcove, and kitchen room-divider.

Horizontal cedar walls in a family room

groove of this new strip onto the tongue of the first board. Use a piece of scrap paneling with a groove in it for this job, by placing the groove up against the tongue of the new board and hammering it in with the scrap. Fasten succeeding boards in position by toenailing through the base of the projecting tongue. Don't face-nail the boards except for the first and last ones on each wall.

Horizontal boards and new plywood facings, of course, involve exactly the opposite method of construction. The supports must be vertical to the ceiling, so the wall-studs have to be located without tearing out the old inner walls.

Magnetic Stud-finder

Trying to find a stud in a wall can be a frustrating experience. The rapping technique frequently yields nothing more than sore knuckles. The alternative, drilling a series of holes until you finally hit a stud by luck, leaves behind a series of holes that must be patched. The magnetic stud-finder can do the job with unerring accuracy; slide it along the wall until

Unique horizontal shelving boards

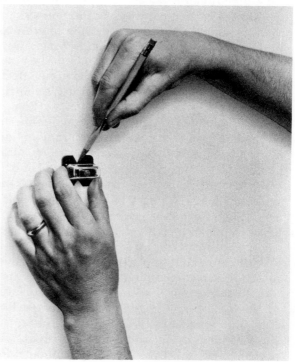
Magnetic stud-finder

the moving magnet signals that you are right over the nails driven into a stud. Start at the baseboards, where stud nails are most likely to be found.

Movable Storage Wall

This cleverly constructed wall on casters can be moved from one part of the room to another, to act as a room divider, doorway-entrance vestibule (with a clothes closet to one side), or a wall cabinet. It contains, or can be constructed to contain, according to the accompanying plans, a desk, unique horizontal-board supports for adjustable shelves, tape recorder, phonograph-record storage, filing unit, drawers, and other features. (See Acknowledgments to obtain plans for this storage wall.)

Movable storage wall

7
Putting Up Partition Walls with Doors

The vertical members that support the walls of the house are called studs (numbered 1 on photo). Generally they are made of 2x4 lumber, as are most other matching parts of the walls. Although it's possible to save a bit of money by using 2x3 studs, it is not a good idea. From the standpoint of reinforcement, 2x3 studs are almost as sturdy, but this kind of economy can cause trouble later. For example, built-in gadgets such as cabinets are designed to be installed between the studs. If you use 2x3s instead of 2x4s, the walls won't be thick enough to hold these. That's why 2x4s have become the universally preferred size for interior walls.

Some lumberyards will allow you to pick out your material from their stacks. If you can do this, it is recommended. If you can't, check over the lumber when it is delivered and reject any lengths that are badly damaged or twisted. If you are a regular customer, the lumber company will replace them with better stock. However, don't expect perfection from the grade-C lumber you will use inside of walls (see Chapter 11).

Try to order your lumber in lengths that you can cut to the size you need with a minimum of waste. Usually, this means 2x4s in either 8- or 16-foot lengths (most ceilings are now 8 feet high). To a certain extent, waste is unavoidable. No matter how carefully you plan your work, you're bound to wind up with a stack of small wood chunks. Save every piece of finished lumber. There are a thousand uses for it, from making under-deck block supports (cleats) to making children's toy blocks. The cost of milled lumber has now reached such a level that the old habit of using scraps for firewood no longer seems tolerable.

If you live in the East, chances are the 2x4s you order will be fir. In the West, they're likely to be redwood. Either of these are perfectly fine woods for your purpose. (See Chapter 11). If they have been stacked properly in the lumberyard, they are likely to be relatively straight and free from warp. Both woods will hold nails well without splitting too easily.

Although putting up a stud-wall is a task that goes swiftly, as a general rule, take the time to get accurate measurements. Also make certain that the whole construction is both level and square. It will only take a few minutes during this phase of the job, and it will save a great deal of time when you put up the inside wall-panels.

Planning and Layout

Here's the step-by-step procedure for erecting interior stud-walls. Since you will probably be involved in a remodeling job, the new wall will most likely hook into the existing structure of the house. Following your plans or sketches, measure along the existing wall to the point where the new partition should jut off. Drive a nail partway into the floor at this exact spot. Fasten one end of a chalk-line with an awl or nail and stretch the line out in the direction that the partition will extend. Line up a carpenter's square so that one leg touches the nail and one leg is flush with the existing wall. Hold the square firmly in position while your assistant moves the string back and forth until it lines up perfectly with the leg of the square. When the taut string is exactly aligned, snap it to make a chalk-mark extending across the floor.

Place a 2x4 flat-side down on the floor and line it up perfectly with the chalk-mark. This piece of lumber is called the shoe or sole-plate (labeled 2 in illustration), and it forms the base of the partition. Later the upright studs will be nailed to it. Fasten the shoe to the floor with 16d nails placed about 16 inches apart. Usually, when nails are to be positioned along a straight run of wood such as this, it's standard building practice to stagger them — that is, hammer them down off-center, alternating with one nail toward one side of the shoe and one toward the other, so there will be no tendency for them to split the wood.

If the partition includes a doorway, don't bother about cutting the part of the shoe that extends across the future doorway opening. It's much easier to remove the section of the shoe that's in the way later.

Cut the first 2x4 (marked 3 in the illustration) so that it will fit on top of the shoe and extend to the future ceiling-plate. Fasten it to the wall on top of the shoe at the point where

1. Studs 2. Shoe or sole plate 3. First stud vertical along corner 4. Ceiling-stud, or plate 5. Blind-studs 6. Studs marked on shoe exactly 16 inches apart, center to center 7. Furring strips

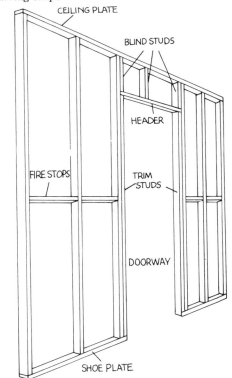

Diagram of wall construction

Scratch-awl. The chalk-line is used for long straight lines. Be sure to snap the taut line square to the surface.

the shoe joins the existing wall. Using the carpenter's level, make sure this end-stud is vertical before you spike it in place. This piece of wood forms the end nailing surface for the wall-panels when they are applied later to all the studs.

Make a mark on the upright where the 8-foot ceiling will be, exactly in line with the outer edge of the 2x4 that you've nailed to the wall. The best way to determine this is with a carpenter's square. Hold it so the inner edge of the 24-inch leg rests against the upright 2x4. The end of the leg will indicate the ceiling placement. Make a pencil-mark along the inside edge of the long leg. This mark locates the position of the horizontal timber that will be nailed to the upright. (Note that the roofline in the room in the illustration is slanting.)

The ceiling-stud (marked 4 in the illustration) is called a plate. All the vertical studs will extend between the shoe and the plate. The short studs between the plate and the roofbeam (marked 5 in the illustration) are called blind studs, and they will be nailed in later. Cut the 2x4 for the plate the same length as the shoe, and fasten it on top of the first stud. Use only one nail for this job, and hammer it in place to the existing end-wall. At this point, although one end of the plate is now fastened to the end-wall, the other end is still movable. As a matter of fact, you will need an assistant to support the other end against the far wall to keep it from falling.

Select a relatively straight 2x4 for the next step. The pool-hall technique is the easiest way to do this: squint one eye and sight along the edge of the 2x4 to see if it is straight. Cut the 2x4 long enough to extend between the floor and the top of the plate or ceiling-stud of the room, minus 1 inch.

Note that this 2x4 will be used as a measuring stud for all the others, and it is not going to be nailed to the plate, so don't measure the distance from the ceiling-plate to the shoe to get the correct length for the studs. This particular stud will rest on the floor alongside the shoe and extend up to the ceiling alongside the plate. You'll use this end stud to locate the far end of the plate that is held by your assistant in position so that, when you fasten the

plate on top of the other studs, it will be exactly in line with the shoe on the floor. Here's how to do that.

Place the upright stud so that one end of it rests against the side of the shoe. Hold it in place firmly with your foot. Now rest the top edge of it against the side of the loose end of the plate.

Hold the level against the side of the upright measuring stud and move the measuring stud and the plate up and down until the bubble in the carpenter's level is centered, indicating that the plate is level. Nail the loose end of the plate to the wall. The plate is now perfectly in line with the shoe on the floor. It's a good idea to mark the straight stud and save it, in case you have to perform this maneuver again and also to insure that all your studs are the same.

You will now cut all the vertical studs to fit exactly between the shoe and the plate, and will position them a standard 16 inches apart, center to center. The short leg of your carpenter's square (16 inches long) is designed for this calculation. However, don't mark where the center of the stud will hit and try to line it up perfectly on this single mark. Instead mark off the thickness of the studs on the shoe so you can set each stud within the area you have outlined (labeled 6 in the illustration).

To accomplish this, place the carpenter's square on the shoe with the narrow leg hanging over one side. Press this narrow leg up against the shoe so the thick leg will be perpendicular to the wood. Then simply make a pencil-mark on either side of the thick leg. Those two marks indicate the exact thickness of the vertical studs. Repeat the same routine all along the shoe.

Measure the distance between the plate on the ceiling and the shoe on the floor. If you are in luck, they may all be of equal length. In this event, you can trim all the studs to length at the same time. To do this, line the studs up on the floor with a 2x4 under one end to raise them, measure and mark them, and then zip across your markings with a hand electric-saw.

This sounds too easy? You're right; in most cases, it won't be this simple, because few houses are really plumb level or square. You will probably have to measure and cut each stud individually for its place along the shoe and plate, because each will probably have to differ slightly in length.

One at a time, nail the studs first to the shoe and then to the plate. The traditional method is to toenail them into place using two nails on each side of the stud, driving them in at an angle. You'll find the job a little easier if you drive one nail in on one side, then one on the other; then go back to the first side and drive in the second nail and finally the second nail on the remaining side.

No matter how firmly you try to hold the stud in place against the shoe, it will have a tendency to move when you hammer the nails in. This back and forth hammering will make it easier to position the individual studs accurately on the plate.

After a stud is secured to the shoe, place your carpenter's level vertically against it. Rock the stud and level back and forth slightly until the bubble in the level is centered. Mark the position of the upper end of the stud on the plate. Toenail the top end of the stud to the plate as you did with the shoe.

Fire-stops

It's good standard building practice to put in fire-stops. These are simply short 2x4s nailed horizontally between the studs about halfway up from the floor. They are a safety precaution and add no structural strength. Without fire-stops, the hollow interior of the walls of a house could act as a chimney in case of a fire, drawing the flames up inside the wall. A fire-stop simply shortens the unobstructed run of the hollow space and greatly minimizes this flue action.

Utilize odds-and-ends of short lumber for this. You will find it easier to put them all in at one time after the studding is up. Saw the fire-stops to the proper lengths, and nail them in place through the vertical studs on either side of the blocks. There is also a metal framing-bracket called a back-up clip that you can buy to support them firmly (see page 46).

You will find that the job will be easier if you stagger the fire-stops slightly so that alternate ones are a little higher. Then you'll always be able to nail directly through a stud into the

block. Otherwise one side of a stud will always be blocked by the previous fire-stop.

There is no need for fire-stops in outside walls that are fiberglass-insulated. (The wall in the illustration is an outside wall, so it has no fire-stops. The diagram of an inner wall has fire-stops.)

Metal-connectors and Anchors

A method easier than toenailing is using preformed framing-anchors. These are ingenious thin steel connectors used for joining any two wood members — a stud against the shoe, a stud against the plate, or any other nailing surfaces. "Anchors" can be used in building a house as well as in merely fastening a stud or framing a doorway. These gadgets are considered by many people to give a much stronger joint than toenailing; and they have been used in tornado and earthquake country because they strengthen a structure vertically as well as horizontally. (See page 58.)

Door Openings

If your studding line includes a door opening, here's how to frame it. Measure up from the floor to the top of the door opening — traditionally 6 feet 8 inches. However, determine this by the height of the door you are going to install. Be sure to allow for such items as new flooring, trim, and the like. Cut out the doorway shoe. Instead of a single stud on either side of the opening, nail a second stud called the "trim-stud" side-by-side with the studs on either side of the opening where the door will be. In other words, double up on the studding to the height of the door. These double studs together make up one heavier timber for the door-frame.

Fasten the trim studs to the shoe and stud in the doorway in exactly the same manner as you nailed down the single studs, but note that the trim-studs reach to the floor.

Attach a double 2x4 stud — called the header — to the vertical stud across the top of the doorway to be nailed down to the trim-stud. In the space on top of the door-frame extending

Four different wall-connectors

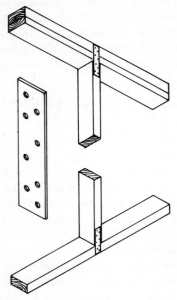

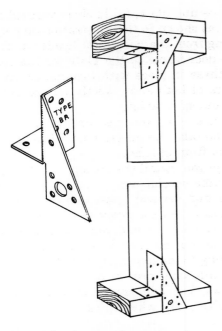

Strap between header and stud or shoe and stud

Framing-anchor between plate and stud or stud and shoe (version 1)

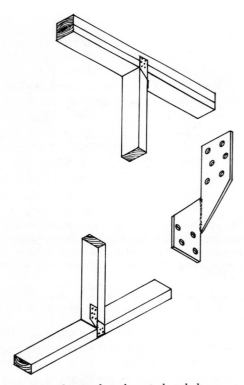

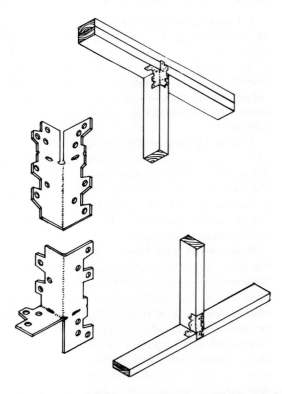

Anchor between plate and stud or stud and shoe

Framing-anchor between plate and stud or stud and shoe (version 2)

to the ceiling-plate, fill in short vertical blind-studs (as shown in the illustration on page 55) running from the horizontal header at the top of the door-frame to the plate for the ceiling. Hold these in place with toenails or framing-anchors at both ends exactly as you did with the standard studding.

Be sure when you measure the door height that you take the measurement from the floor and not from the shoe.

When you install the inside trim-stud for the door, take special care to make it absolutely square and vertical, with wood-shingles used as shims to get the doorway 90-degrees vertical. If you don't, when you install the door itself, you will have to do a lot of unnecessary trimming to make it hang properly.

Use this same procedure for framing around windows, but add short vertical blind-studs both above the window-frame and below the sill-stud.

Installing a Pre-hung Door and a Pre-hung Window

All doors, whether interior or exterior, and all windows can be ordered pre-hung, ready to install. Or they may be bought without frames of any kind. Of course, the latter are less expensive, but — whether working with a carpenter or not — the amateur saves much labor by installing pre-hung doors and windows.

The term "pre-hung" means that it has all trim — including the ¾-inch wood-jamb that fits against the 2x4 studs and the outer facing that shows both inside and outside the wall. It is necessary to know the precise dimensions of the pre-hung door or window to make the door- and window-openings fit.

If you want trim that is not obtainable with the door or window, or if you do not want to pay the extra price, you can — with the simplest of tools — cut the jambs that are nailed to the rough double 2x4 frame. The jambs may be simple ¾x4 boards, surmounted by ½-inch inner-moldings against which the door will close. Then, around the outside of the door or window, you can mount moldings that suit your architecture — plain or as deeply molded as a picture-frame.

Again, you can use the metal connectors, called shims, that will make the job easy. If you have not bought a pre-hung door (or window) with all the hardware previously installed by the manufacturer, all the above is simple compared to preparing the door for hanging.

Hanging an Unprepared Door

There are several kinds of stock doors available from lumberyards. Heaviest and sturdiest is the solid-core flush-door. Much the same in appearance but much lighter in weight is a honeycomb flush-door. The inside of it looks like a jumbo separater from an egg-crate. There are also the more traditional paneled doors. Select one sized to your door-opening or slightly larger.

The standard interior-door height is 6 feet 8 inches, with widths varying from 2 feet to 3 feet; usually 2 feet 4 inches, 2 feet 6 inches, or 2

Metal shims for installing pre-hung doors

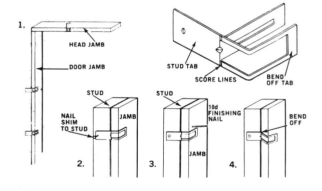

1. Install metal shims along one side and top of jamb by sliding U-shaped "bend-off" portion over the edge of newly fitted, not yet nailed jamb. Be sure shims are pushed fully "home" against the edge of jamb. Use four equi-distant shims on each side jamb and one shim on the head jamb.

2. Check again for plumb and squareness. Nail metal shims to edge of studs through precut hole. Use 6d common wire nails.

3. Nail jambs just above bend-off tab to face of studs and header using 10d nails.

4. After all jambs have been nailed to the studs, break off "bend-off" tab of metal shims at the score line.

A.

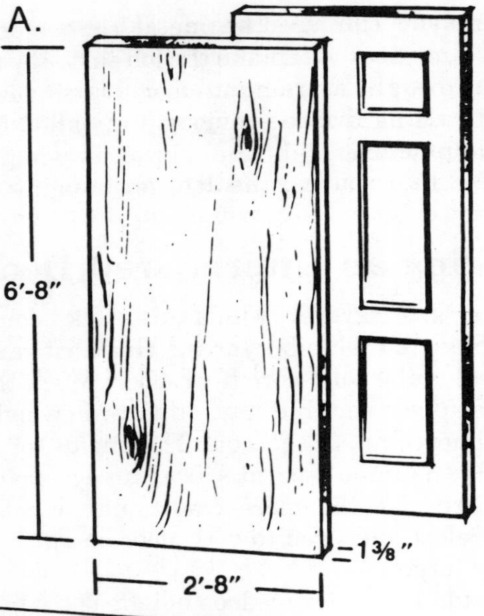

B.

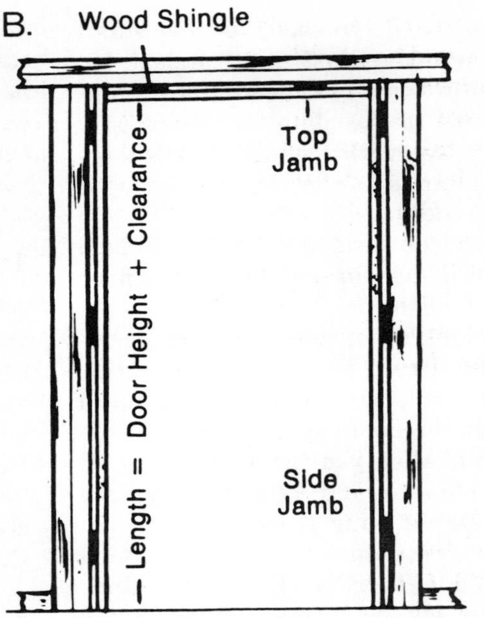

C.

D.

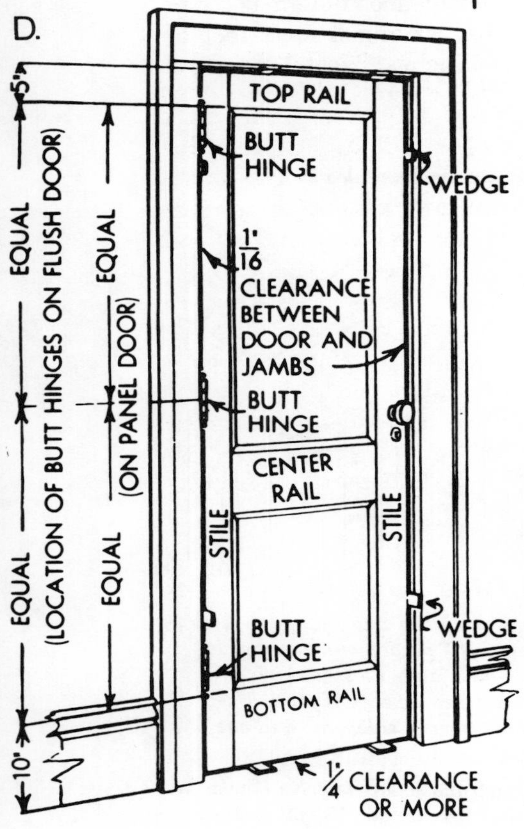

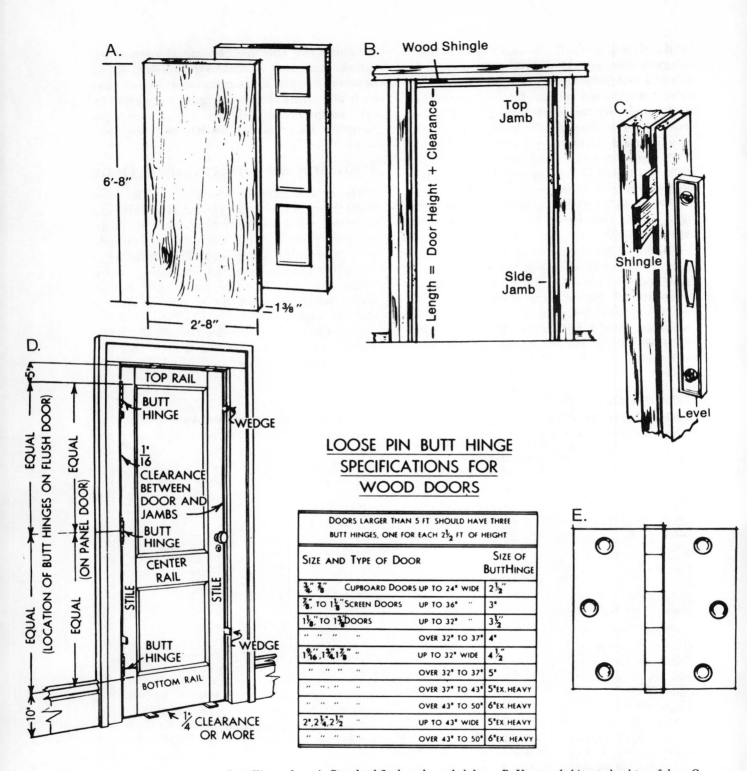

LOOSE PIN BUTT HINGE SPECIFICATIONS FOR WOOD DOORS

Doors larger than 5 ft should have three butt hinges, one for each 2½ ft of height

Size and Type of Door		Size of Butt Hinge
¾″ ⅞″ Cupboard Doors	up to 24″ wide	2½″
⅞″ to 1⅛″ Screen Doors	up to 36″ ″	3″
1⅛″ to 1⅜″ Doors	up to 32″ ″	3½″
″ ″ ″ ″	over 32″ to 37″	4″
1 9/16″, 1¾″, 1⅞″ ″	up to 32″ wide	4½″
″ ″ ″ ″	over 32″ to 37″	5″
″ ″ ″ ″	over 37″ to 43″	5″ ex. heavy
″ ″ ″ ″	over 43″ to 50″	6″ ex. heavy
2″, 2¼″, 2½″ ″	up to 43″ wide	5″ ex. heavy
″ ″ ″ ″	over 43″ to 50″	6″ ex. heavy

E.

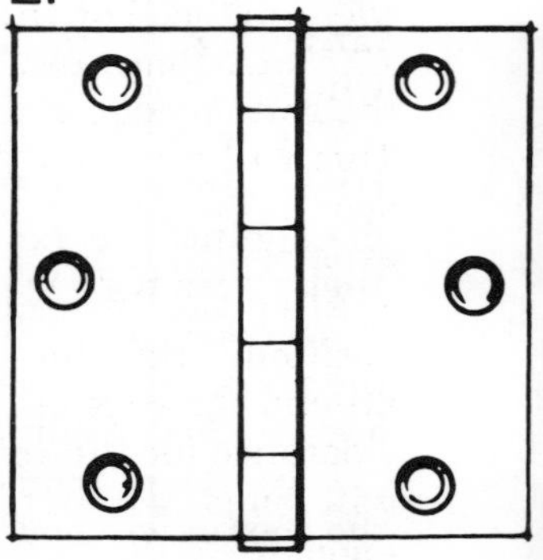

Installing a door. A: Standard flush and paneled doors. B: Use wood shims to level top of door. C: Use wood shims to get 90-degree-angle casing, using level. D: Terms used for installing panel or flush-door, with hinge sizes. E: For installing hinges, see how to chisel the gain (or inset) for butt door-hinge, page 91.

feet 8 inches is used. Double-doors are of course narrower (the standard widths are 1 foot ⅜ inch or 1 foot ¾ inch), and in pairs a great deal wider, as two are needed for each doorway. Four panels are needed if each pair is folded back for still wider, grander doorways.

For the most part, solid-core and paneled doors will give you more leeway in trimming them down to fit the opening. It's impossible to slice inches off a honeycomb flush-door. If you cut too deeply, you may go right through the solid rim of the door into the interior honeycomb section.

Many doors are supplied from the lumberyard with side-rails projecting beyond the bottom of the door. Saw these off flush and then place the door against the opening so you can see how much of the door should be removed.

If only a light trimming is needed, use a jack-plane for the job. (Using the shorter plane may leave the door with an uneven wavy surface.) If ½ inch or more of wood has to be cut off, use a saw and then the plane.

Cut down one edge and the top of the door until you can slip it partly into the opening. Scribe the remaining edge with a pencil, using the door-jamb as a guide. Once you've removed this wood, you should be able to fit the door entirely into the frame.

The next step is to trim the door slightly more so as to allow enough clearance all the way around. For this operation, you will need 15 cents. Place two nickels on the floor under the bottom edge of the door (¼-inch clearance). This will give you the upper clearance. If the door has to open over a rug, you'll have to cut it even shorter and fit a threshold in beneath it.

After the two nickels and the door are in position, slide the third nickel all the way around the edge of the door. If there is enough clearance for the coin to move freely, the door will open without binding. If there is not enough clearance, trim the door down very gradually with a plane.

Now attach the hinges. The modern trend is to use three hinges on a door instead of the traditional two. This supports the weight better and gives the door a smoother action.

Position the top hinge about 7 inches from the top of the door and the bottom one 11 inches from the floor. The third hinge goes halfway between these two. Hinges are set into a shallow mortise cut in the narrow edge of the door. The depth of the mortise equals the thickness of one hinge-leaf.

Support the door hinge-side up on the floor, and place the three hinges on top in the proper position. The edge of the hinge-leaf on the opposite side from the hinge-pin should be about $1/16$ inch from the edge of the door. The rest of the hinge (the part with the hinge-pin) overhangs. Mark the position of the hinges on the door with a sharp chisel. Then use a hammer and chisel to cut out the mortise for each hinge (as described on page 91).

Check your work frequently by fitting the hinge-leaves back into place. When they fit flush with the surface of the wood, drill $1/16$-inch holes about ½ inch deep to act as pilot-holes for the screws.

Slip the door back into the opening. Make sure that it's aligned in the correct position (get your nickels out again), and then mark on the jamb where the hinges will be fastened. Remove the door, separate the two halves of the three hinges by pulling out the hinge-pins. Chisel out the three mortises in the door-jamb and mount the hinge-leaves in place.

Place the door back into the opening, interlocking the leaves of the hinges. Fit the pins into place, starting at the top hinge and working down. Check to see that the door opens and closes without binding. If the door binds on the lock side, insert cardboard shims under the hinges to lift them out of the mortises slightly.

Installing Doorknobs and Latches

If the door has not been purchased with the doorknob and its mechanism already installed, there's a bit of delicate carpentry to attend to. A standard cylindrical lock or a mortise lock may be bought from a locksmith. At the suitable lock height (usually 36 inches from the floor), mark a line at the center of the door-edge and — using the combination square — mark a vertical and a horizontal line across the front of the door; then mark the horizontal line with the square a few inches along both sides of the

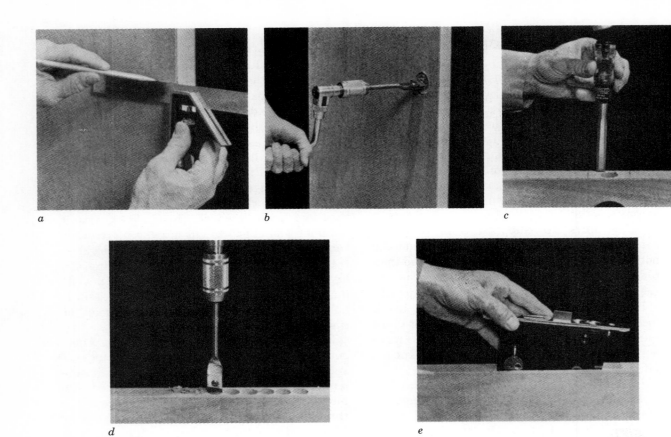

a

b

c

d

e

door (illustration a). To get the doorknob and latch into the door for the lock, bore a hole with an expansion bit (see Chapter 10, page 94). Be sure not to bore all the way through the door; it will cause a rough edge on the opposite side. When the tip of the bit comes through, stop and bore the hole from the other side. This hole is for the doorknob (illustration b).

Next, at the edge of the door, carefully bore a hole in the edge of the door into the large hole, and then chisel out a thin strip where the facing of the cylindrical lock will be inserted to fit flush with the wood. Carefully chisel the thin facing in the front of the door where the latch will fit (illustration c). Follow the instructions of the manufacturer for this kind of key in the knob lock.

For a mortise lock of an exterior door, follow the manufacturer's template or pattern to bore a series of holes in the edge of the door for the lock (illustration d). Leave about ⅛ inch

between the holes just to the depth of the mortise lock, which will slip in after you have made an oblong opening with hammer and chisel where the bit-holes were. The depth of the hole will, of course, be the depth of the mortise lock. The mortise lock should fit perfectly into the opening (illustration e). Screw the plates on the front and back of the door, and into the lock at the edge of the door. Remove the lock, and mark on the door the openings for the key cylinder and doorknob spindle as indicated by the manufacturer's template and instructions.

There are several different types of door locks and latches on the market. All of them come complete with templates and instructions. Just make sure the lock you buy is designed to fit the thickness of the door you are using. Following the manufacturer's instructions, use the templates provided to install the lock.

Finishing the Door

Nail the trim in place on the jamb. As a last step in fitting the door, fasten the door-stop molding to the jamb. This is the narrow strip, usually 2 to 4 inches, on the inside door opening that prevents the door from swinging too far into the opening. For the sake of appearance, and to seal off the door in the frame, this stop is carried all the way around the two sides and top of the jamb. Hold it in place with small finishing-nails set below the surface of the wood.

The door should be flush, when closed, with the trim that you choose to give a finished look on the wall around the door. Some people prefer a contemporary look with no trim at all, leaving the door flush with the wall.

8
Refinishing Wood Floors and Ceilings

Preparations are important. If the existing floor is not level and smooth, it is essential that you either sand it flat or else put down plywood subflooring to bridge any irregularities.

Have the floorboards delivered about a week before you plan to lay them. They will then have the chance to expand or contract and adjust themselves to normal house temperature. If you lay them when they are full of moisture, they will gradually shrink until cracks appear between them.

To clear an old floor, just sweep it well. If necessary, rent a floor sanding machine and grind down lumps or imperfections. (But amateurs should be careful not to gouge holes in soft-wood subfloors.) Nail down loose boards before sanding. Hammer down projecting nails. The floor should be level and relatively smooth, but it doesn't have to have a glassy surface to serve as a subfloor.

Remove all the trim and molding from around the edge. Since you will probably install new molding, just rip up the old stuff. On the other hand, if you plan to put back the original material, pry it up very carefully using a wide chisel levered against a small block of wood. Remove all old nails from the molding from the back with the least damage possible.

It's poor economy to use anything but hardwood flooring, though some people prefer the warm grain of pine, giving it a hard surface with a translucent polyethylene coat. (Fabulon gives pine floors, old or new, a good hard finish.) All pre-milled flooring sold in strips is tongue-and-groove material. A projecting lip on one board fits into a groove cut into the second board. When properly installed, the boards hold together as a unit. In addition to the tongue and groove running along the edges of the boards, some hardwood flooring also comes with the same kind of mill-work on the ends so that these as well as the sides lock together.

If the existing flooring is in such bad shape that it is too unstable a base for a new floor, professionals always nail or fasten down 4x8 plywood subflooring on top of the old, carefully fitting it over the entire floor. There is a utility material intended for this purpose. It will be rough-sanded, with knots and imperfections on both sides. Don't despair and don't repair. These do not reduce the structural strength of the plywood at all, but do cut your costs by a gratifying amount.

Hardwood flooring with redwood plywood wall-paneling

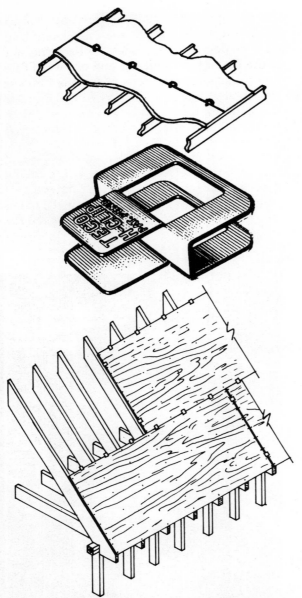

H-clips for fastening 4x8-foot plywood sheet subflooring and roofing

Use plenty of nails to fasten down the plywood sheets. Depending on the condition of the existing floor, you can use either ¼-inch or ⅜-inch-thick plywood. Fastening the sheets with coated nails or ring-nails, space about 10 inches apart around the edges and down the center of each sheet.

The job will go much faster, with a minimum of nailing and a maximum of strength, if you use the metal connectors now available.

H-clips are made especially to hold 4x8 plywood flooring and roofing firmly together regardless of where the joints are. So, if your roof has rotted, you can tear out the bad sections and use plywood sheets held by H-clips in the same manner as you do a floor (without tearing out the old surface).

Check the floor surface for springiness and, if necessary, nail loose boards to the joists below. You may have to use longer nails to drive through the plywood and old flooring into the joists below.

Place strips of building-felt from wall to wall across the plywood panels or subfloor. The edges of the strips should overlap by about 4 inches. Use a type known as 15-pound asphalt felt. (Just ask for it by this name at the building-supply company. They will know what you mean.) The purpose of this felt layer is to seal off the subfloor to keep dirt from seeping up through the joints and to eliminate any possibility of drafts coming up through the boards. There's no need to nail down the felt. Just unroll it on the floor in long strips. The finished flooring will hold it in place.

Flooring generally comes in random lengths. Sort out the long boards and use them where their appearance counts. Save the short cut-off lengths for halls, closets, and other small spaces. It's a good idea to lay the floor at a right angle to the subfloor beneath. However, if you are using a plywood subfloor, plan so that the finished boards run at right angles to the joists beneath. Then you can nail through the finished boards and plywood subflooring into the joists.

As with wall-paneling, the first strip is the most critical. This is the one that goes against the wall. First measure and cut to the proper length (though it will probably not run the full length of the room). Then position the strip ¼ inch away from the wall. The grooved edge of the board should face the wall, with the tongue-edge facing out into the room. Be sure to leave the ¼-inch gap between the first board and the wall. It's there to allow for possible expansion of the board. If you put the floor firmly up against the walls, it will buckle if the wood swells.

Drive the first row of nails through the board along the edge facing the wall. You will have to use a nail-set to drive the nail-head through the surface of the board, but don't fret. The nail-holes will later be hidden by shoe-molding.

Use 10d nails for this first strip, and space them so they can be driven directly into the joists beneath.

After you have nailed down the side of the board that is facing the wall, nail down the tongue-edge of the same board. (This is the surface that faces out into the room.) These nails should go in at about a 45-degree angle. Drive them through the base of the tongue. Don't try to drive the nail all the way in, however. Pound in the last ½ inch or so using a nail-set. This way you will avoid marring the wood with the hammer.

This process of nailing through the projecting tongue of the board is called "blind-nailing." When you fasten the next board into place, with its groove overlapping the tongue of the first board, the nails will be completely hidden.

Don't skimp on nailing. It may take a little more time now; but, if you do the job properly and carefully, you will have a squeak-free floor.

Measure and cut for the second board, and place it against the first one with the tongue and groove interlocking. As you fit each board beside the preceding one, draw them firmly together. The procedure for this is exactly the same as that used for the vertical wood-paneling (see pages 51 to 52).

Use a piece of scrap flooring and place it so the groove of the scrap fits over the tongue of the last floorboard. Hammer on the outer edge of the scrap to drive the floorboard into position. This maneuver keeps you from chewing up the finished floor. Don't hit so hard as to damage the tongue or the groove.

The boards will not be fitted in precise parallel lengths. Stagger the joints at the ends of the board so they are at least a foot longer or shorter in succeeding rows. Also make sure that all the joints at the ends of boards occur over joists.

If your flooring is tongue-and-grooved on the ends of the boards as well as on the sides, blind-nail them through the tongue, and interlock the tongue-grooves just as you did the sides of the boards. However, if your flooring

has straight ends on it, simply butt the two firmly together. Toenail the end of one board on a 45-degree angle, then nail-set the nails of the board that abuts it, and use wood-filler. End tongue-and-groove is, of course, the best.

Although you've nailed down the first strip through the face of the wood, all succeeding strips are nailed only through the projecting tongue.

This holds true until you've worked your way across the room. When you're fitting the last floorboard into place, it will be impossible to toenail it. Working so close to the wall, you just won't have room to swing a hammer. So face-

nail this last strip, forcing it as tightly as you can against the previous one. For a neater job, you can use finishing-nails along this last row, sinking them slightly below the surface with a nail-set.

Fit the boards very carefully under door-frames and moldings, and around any irregularities in the room. If you have a house with very ornate moldings around the door that can't be taken up, this can be a very tricky procedure.

However, there is an easy way out. Instead of trying to fit the floorboards to the intricate curve of the molding, just saw the molding off at the very bottom. Then you can slip the floorboards beneath. To do this, place a floorboard up against the molding, and rest a fine-tooth saw flat on the board. Work very slowly as you cut through the molding. The

floorboard, combined with the thickness of the saw-teeth, will act as a gauge, and you will have just enough room to slip the new flooring beneath the cut section.

New techniques have changed the finishing of ceilings more than any other part of the house, but the householder seems to be a little bashful about taking full advantage of them. Totally new effects are possible inexpensively; and they can be put up by the do-it-yourself amateur, including suspended ceilings, ornamental tiles, acoustical tiles, and gypsum wallboard (no longer the nightmare it once was; see Chapter 6).

And there is also wood-paneling and interesting board effects that will draw the eye to the ceiling rather than to the floor (so often wall-to-wall carpeted) or to the walls (so often

First act for a suspended ceiling

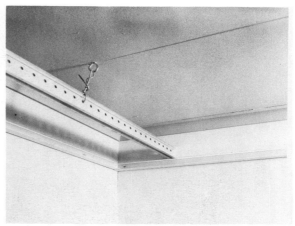

The first runner

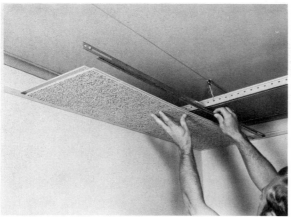

The first 4-foot cross-tee

The ceiling rapidly expands, without a seam.

A second method is attaching tees to clips on beams.

Ceiling channels are easiest – even 1-foot panels are interlocked.

Traditional elegance, in a matter of hours

glassed or shelved). At the same time, it is becoming more usual to find beams and lighting in panels overhead.

With the new suspended ceilings, no supports are visible. The first step is to nail a strong molding to all four walls at the desired ceiling height (double ceilings are the answer in this new method).

The first runner is located 26 inches from wall to wall, and others are added across the room at 48-inch intervals — forming strong but light beams suspended from the ceiling.

Four-foot cross-tees are snapped to the main runners, and the first tiles (four-footers) are slid into concealed slots. The process is con-

tinued across the room, each tile fitted into the next under the cross-tees, so that no seam is evident anywhere on the ceiling. The whole process is simple and fast.

If the ceiling has exposed joists or unsightly beams, the attachment to the ceiling becomes even more simple because there is no need to locate firm ceiling positions for the main runners. (These are usually located with a stud-finder; see Chapter 6.) Simple metal clips fasten the tees to the joists.

Another, perhaps simpler, method of installation is to nail wood or metal firring channels at the molding and on the ceiling and hang the cross-tees from them. These can support 4-foot tiles, and also interlocking foot-square tiles, which give a different decorative effect.

An amazing variety of designs can be accomplished in this simple installation. Shown here is the effect of a plaster-relief ceiling that can measure up to the elegance of Colonial Williamsburg. Of course, you have to have the interior to go with it. Plainer walls and simpler modern apartment windows can be complemented by a well-chosen design in the ceiling. A noisy family room with rough-pine panel-walls can benefit from acoustical tiles. And some of the panels can be left out to make room for fluorescent lighting.

It is also effective to wallpaper the ceiling, cement light tiles (if the plasterboard is firm), or create fabric canopies by stapling inexpensive fabric. And there will always be great appeal in plain white overhead, setting off wallpaper or pictures on the walls.

Unique treatment of hallway with exposed ceiling beams.

9
Windows and Outer Doors

The variety and range of windows and window units is enough to confound even an architect. If you are seeking unusual effects or odd shapes, a glazier will have to be brought in. Needless to say, that's expensive, but it may be worth it to gain the individuality you want. In any case, the major part of your job will be hunting down the right windows that come finished in their frames, needing only the right-size opening in the wall to install.

The same is true of doors.

Space here permits us to deal only with installation, and we advise the amateur to stick to pre-finished doors and windows. You can still achieve individual effects: in the illustration opposite, you can see the end of a series of small kitchen windows, a skylight, and — in the living room — a wall of panel-windows floor to ceiling (some of which open), an entryway with panel-windows, and (just visible) a sliding glass door. Most are framed and trimmed inside and out. Note, however, as cautioned in Chapter 7, that the shed-roof room containing the window-wall, and opening off a cathedral ceiling, has wood-posts to hold up the main part of the building. Without these, or without crossbeams, that glass wall could not support the outward thrust of the main roof, so choose the location of your window-walls carefully.

Triangular windows are either custom-built or installed in individual framing by a glazier, and they don't open. (Remember this if you are one of those people who prefer fresh air to conditioned air.) The room illustrated here is unique, custom-built.

In these days of fuel shortages, it's a good idea to consider insulated (double) glass, which comes pre-finished in dozens of forms, with instructions for installing.

The sliding glass door has become most popular. As with a regular doorway (Chapter 7), the new opening must fit the door ordered, though more than one or two wall-studs will probably have to be removed and a heavier header used to support the weight of the roof or second floor at that point.

Installing a door, window, or sliding glass doors is an easy job for the amateur because they all come pre-hung from the factory. If you wish to install a fixed plate-window or thermopane (double glass frame to prevent heat loss), it is advisable to attempt to have these framed as well, to avoid the danger of

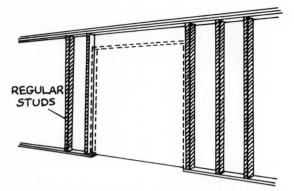

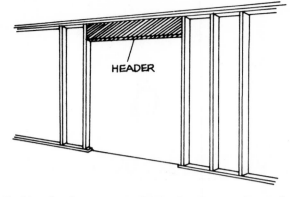

Lay out sliding-door opening width between regular studs to equal the sliding-door rough-opening width plus the thickness of two regular studs.

Position header at proper height between regular studs. Nail through regular studs into header to hold in place until completing next step.

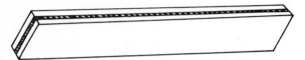

Cut two pieces of header material – these are two 2 x 12s – to equal the rough-opening width of sliding door plus the thickness of two studs. Nail two header members together using adequate spacer so header thickness equals width of stud. Your lumber dealer will advise you the size of the header according to the span of the wide glass doors.

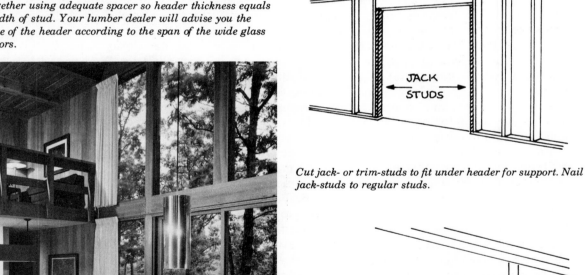

Cut jack- or trim-studs to fit under header for support. Nail jack-studs to regular studs.

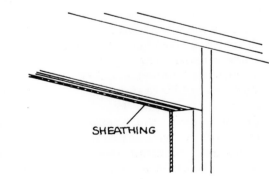

Apply exterior sheathing (fiberboard, plywood, etc.) flush with the header and stud framing-members.

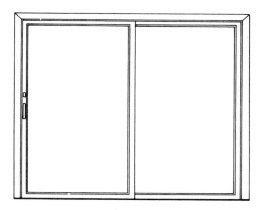

The sliding glass door (which can open left or right depending on where the handle is put), comes with the frame to fit into the wall-opening (which must be leveled and squared!). Different manufacturers will have different instructions for installation.

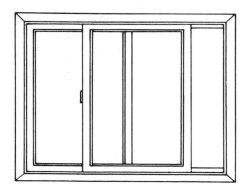

The sliding glass window is constructed in almost the fashion as the sliding door, with a wide variety of shapes, but the screening is always on the outside, and the screen is fixed.

breakage in the handling or installing. Even carpenters may break glass that comes in a single frame without the inside and outside casement when nailing through the thin frame.

When expecting any glass, framed or not, arrange to be there when it arrives. Some truckmen don't think twice about leaving glass, protected only by wood strips and paper covering, leaning against the side of the house, in danger of blowing over from the first strong wind.

It's easiest to install a door where you can take out the frame of a window, having to rip out only the interior and exterior surface below the window, sawing through the wall along the studs or using a ripping hammer for inside and a masonry hammer outside. If removing one stud does not leave you room for a door, remove two studs, being careful not to choose a part of the outside wall that is carrying the weight of the roof, or you will weaken your house structure. Slanting roofs push outward (especially under a snow-load) and depend on second-story floor-joists or ceiling-rafters to hold the walls in place. Where there is a cathedral ceiling (without such joists or raft-

Once the frame is installed, the door is merely lifted into position. It can be taken out as easily for washing. The same is true of sliding glass windows, regardless of size.

ers), if you open up a wall to accommodate a door with matching windows on either side or to make room for two French doors with a fixed picture-window between them, you can so weaken the house that it will literally come tumbling down.

Even where there is no structural danger involved, remember that positioning an outside door or window always affects the exterior architecture and should not be indiscriminately out of line with other doors and windows.

Whatever studs are exposed when the old wall is torn out can be moved to form studs or trim-studs to support the header in the same way they do with an inside door (Chapter 7) and with the sliding glass doors described earlier in this chapter.

If a series of windows is to be installed, the possibility of double-studs between them (never a member as weak as a single stud) will reduce the need for an oversize header, even when six or seven entire walls of windows are involved, as in this house. Here, 4x6 beams are supported across considerable footage by 6x6 uprights and 6x6 beams.

The sliding glass wall in this chapter illustration tells the story. But both amateur and professional must be cautioned to check each fitting while installing, using the carpenter's level at all times. More than one professional has made a frame of trimmer-studs on the sides with header above, only to discover that the house has a slanting floor, and his door-top is not level with the header or the trimmer-studs. Where this is the case, leave the door level at the top, and add shims to fit above the level header. In the end, your ceiling may not be exactly level with the top of the door, but nobody will notice the discrepancy of an inch or so. Whereas if you try to make a crooked door to fit a crooked house, you are not likely to make the proper adjustments.

Nothing is so pleasant or so easy to install as a series of small windows across a room (architecturally, both inside and out, they usually fit) or a large thermopane. Or, if you need a large expanse of glass for an inside garden or collection of plants, you can install a bay-window.

If the joists are at right angles to the wall, for safety's sake, install temporary supports to the ceiling several feet back from the wall—parallel to the windows. If the joists are parallel to the window, no supports are needed.

With sliding glass doors, further care must be taken. Under the door-sill, shims must be carefully placed to make sure that the doors are level. And on either side of the metal grooves that the doors slide through (if that is the style you're using), there must be sills that are slightly higher than the grooves. Otherwise, your family and guests will be continually stepping on the grooves. As they are made of metal softer than steel, you will soon have damaged grooves that require constant straightening with a pair of pliers. Walking on the grooves will also throw the window-frame off-balance, so the doors may not close properly.

The installation should take all hazards into account. Professionals know how to install such valuable doors correctly, even with sliding screens. The amateur should be fully prepared for what is ahead of him so that he will achieve a result that is durable and foolproof. If he does not heed the dangers, he will end up with a sliding door that is hard to slide and will in time fall out of plumb and fail to lock.

One further word: When you order sliding glass doors, order door-handles that will open the door from both inside and outside. Some doors come with an outside door-opener that is an inset you have to move with your finger. If the door falls out of plumb, some member of the family may not have the finger strength to open the door.

You run the same dangers of the house being off-level with your pre-hung window (of whatever type) as you do with doors, so carefully ignore the house's irregularities and simply make the windows level.

Just as you have the simple matter of a door-sill, you have the more complicated question of the window-sill. Be sure to buy a pre-hung window with the window-sill built in; the extra cost of the factory-fashioned frames and sills is worth it if you don't have to measure, level, and improvise.

10
How to Use Hand-tools

Hand-tools are seldom complicated. That's just as well, because it means that using them properly is also likely to be quite simple. However, there is a knack to getting maximum utility with minimum effort out of each one of the basic tools. It takes a little practice in following the instructions that you will find here.

Some of these instructions may repeat points made in the description of these tools in Chapter 3. This is intentional, because these are the most important instructions to absorb. It might be advisable to read the instructions on any one tool in Chapter 3 and Chapter 10 consecutively to be sure you grasp the main points. If you are a beginner, this is your beginner's course. Read and practice before you use a given tool. It will then become second nature.

Hammer

If there is any secret to using a hammer properly, it's this: keep your eye on the head of the nail, not the head of the hammer. Let's see how that works out in actual practice.

First of all, hold the hammer as if you were shaking hands with it. Your grip should be practically flush with the end of the hammer handle. Hold the nail upright with your other hand. Tap it gently to set it into the wood. This maneuver also serves to adjust your aim. When the nail will stand upright on its own, let go and start driving it home.

Vary the force of your wrist and arm according to the size of the nail being hammered. Small nails are tapped in, using a lightweight hammer and wrist-action alone. For a heavier nail, use a heavier hammer and the power of your wrist and arm. For the really big ones, drive them with the full force of your wrist, arm, and shoulder.

Make absolutely certain that when the hammer contacts the nail, the face of the hammer is perfectly perpendicular to the shaft of the nail. This does require practice. However, you can easily tell if you are not doing it correctly: you will bend the nail almost every time.

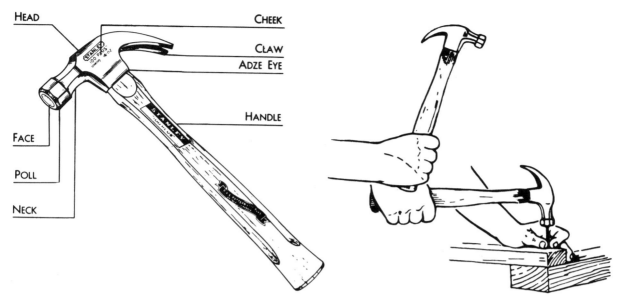

HEAD   CHEEK

CLAW

ADZE EYE

HANDLE

FACE

POLL

NECK

Strike the nail squarely to avoid marring the wood and bending the nail.

Hammer-handles

You will find quite a bit of variation in the material used for the hammer-handles. For many years, hickory wood was traditional. It was tough, and yet had a certain resilience that staved off fatigue. The primary disadvantage was that eventually the head would come loose from the handle; or, under certain circumstances, the handle would splinter. Although wood handles are still being made and sold, most people today prefer either a metal or fiberglass handle. The advantage of these is that the handle is permanently attached.

The choice between metal and fiberglass is a matter of individual preference. Both of these are made with leather or rubber grips that tend to soak up vibration and give a handhold that is relatively slip-proof. Some professional carpenters claim that a fiberglass handle has more of the feel of wood, and they consider this a plus. In all truth, unless you have years of professional experience behind you, you will probably be unable to tell the difference.

Hammer-faces

You will, however, be able to spot the different types of hammer-faces. The face is that flat surface at the end of the head used to drive the nail. A plain face is almost always flat.

Used mostly for house-construction, it does give a little better control in angling nails. Also, because the face is usable all the way out to the edge, you can drive nails in very tight places. However, it does have a tendency to leave hammer-marks on the wood unless you're quite careful.

Your best bet is probably what's called a *bell-face hammer.* It has a little bevel around the edge, and the face, instead of being flat, is very slightly convex. With this combination, you can drive a nail flush with a surface and not leave a hammer-mark. At the same time, you can still angle nails with it, so it's probably your best choice for all-around use.

Avoid a *cross-checkered face.* The patchwork face of this variety would seem to be the ideal choice for a beginner. Logically, the rough face should strike the head of the nail with less tendency for skittering. However, the roughness also leaves a brutal mark on the work-surface. Hammer faces of this type are generally used only for such crude jobs as building crates or the like.

Hammer-claws

Specific signposts of quality include a sharp V-notch between the claws of the hammer. If this surface is not ground to precision, you won't be able to get a good grip on a nail to draw it out. This surfacing should extend all the way up to the apex of the V so that you have the same control with small nails as with large ones.

Metal of Hammer-heads

Check out the tool for indications of the specific metal used to make it. Sometimes this data is stamped right into the hammer itself, but you may also find the information contained on a label or shipping carton. Look for a hammer-head made of drop-forged steel with a hardened head. High-quality hammers are made with different types of tempering. The head is tough, but the body is more resilient, so the tool will withstand impact but not shatter. The same variation exists in the claws, so they will have strength without being brittle.

All these fine points are quite necessary if you are looking for utility and service. A typical hammer-blow carries the impact of 45 foot-pounds. The handle has to take even more strain. If you put 100 pounds of moxie into the job of drawing a nail, that 100 pounds of force at the end of the handle multiplies to something like 1,000 pounds by the time it gets close to the head.

Gadget Hammers

Generally stay away from gadget-type hammers. For a while, there was a fad for hammers with built-in magnets, for example. The purpose was to make it easier to start a nail in an overhead position. According to the theory, you rested the nail in a notch on top of the hammer. Then, in one motion, you could plop the nail into the wood far enough to get it started.

You reversed the hammer to continue driving in the nail the rest of the way. All very fine in theory, but in actual practice repeated blows tended to depower the magnet so that you wound up with just a standard hammer.

One very common error is to "choke" the hammer — that is, to grasp it midway along the handle. Follow this maneuver to its logical conclusion, and you might just as well drive the nail using a rock clenched in your fist.

Sometimes when you are driving a nail into very hard wood, it is necessary to hold the nail when you are hammering the first few blows so that it will stand upright on its own. All too frequently this is an invitation to smashed fingers, but there's an easy way to avoid this. Instead of grasping the nail near the base against the wood, hold it just under the head. If you should miss the nail, there is a good chance that the hammer will merely knock your fingers out of the way instead of smashing them against the board. It may be amateurish, but you can also hold the nail with pliers. Your aim may be better when you have no fear of injury.

For maximum holding-power, try to drive the nail downward at a slight angle. The type of nail you use will have a big effect on how firmly it stays in place. (See Nail Chart, Chapter 11.) Rough surface-nails, either *cement-coated or hot-dipped,* grasp the wood fibers and hang on with an incredible grip. Even better are *ring-nails.* These have a series of grooves running down the shaft of the nail. Driven into place, they tend to lock against the wood-fibers. You get a pretty good idea of how firmly nails stay in position the first time you try to draw one out.

To pull a nail, work the shank of the nail into the V of the hammer claw. Then rock the hammer backward. If you want to avoid marring the surface of the wood, put a fat stick underneath the hammer claw as you pull back, and continue the leverage. If the nail does not come out, place a thicker piece of wood under the hammer for additional leverage. A ripping-bar (see page 23) will furnish the leverage to pull it out if the hammer doesn't.

If a nail should bend while you are driving it in, don't try to straighten it. Instead draw the nail and start over again with a fresh one.

To drive small nails, make a holder from a small strip of scrap cardboard by driving the nail lightly through the cardboard. Hold the nail upright with the cardboard while you tap it smartly. When it will stand upright on its own, pull away the cardboard and keep nailing.

Using the Nail-set

The nail-set is used to drive or set the head of finishing-nails slightly below the surface of the wood. It comes in various sizes to match the nail-heads, and you should make sure that the tip of the nail-set you select is no bigger than

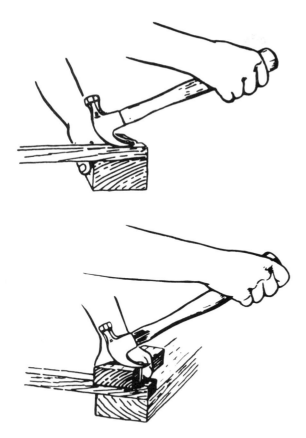

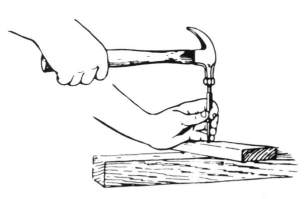

To draw a nail, slip the claw of the hammer under the nail-head; pull until the handle is nearly vertical and the nail partly drawn. To continue the pull, slip a piece of wood under the head of the hammer to increase the leverage and to relieve the unnecessary strain on the handle.

the diameter of the nail-head that you want to drive below the surface. Now here's how you use it. With a hammer, drive the nail down until it is almost flush with the wood. Then, hold the nail-set on the head of the nail. Strike one blow on the other end of the nail set. Check the position of the nail before you hit it again. For best results, the nail should be set below the surface to a distance equal to the diameter of the head. Later, when you are applying paint or finish, you can fill in the small hole with plastic-wood and sand it smooth after it has dried.

It's a small matter, but if you buy a nail-set that has a square top on it, it won't have the tendency to roll away from you every time you put it down.

One special type of nail-set insures against slipping from the nail-head by a cylindrical encasing body, which is struck while the nail-set head remains stationary.

Driver for Corrugated Fasteners

They're sometimes called scotch-nails, but whatever the terminology, corrugated fasteners can do a superb job of holding wooden surfaces together, often much better than nails. Many craftsmen, however, find them difficult to drive home. This gadget simplifies the task considerably and makes it virtually foolproof.

Gadget for driving corrugated nails

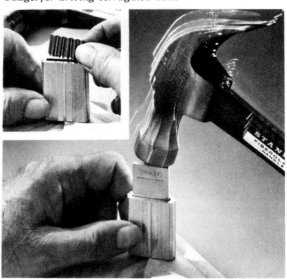

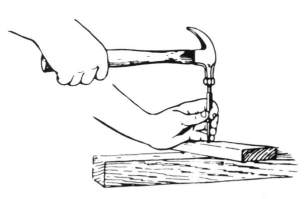

Use a nail-set to drive nails below the surface of all fine work. To prevent the nail-set from slipping off the head of the nail, rest the little finger on the work and press the nail-set firmly against it. Set nails about 1/16 inch below the surface of the wood.

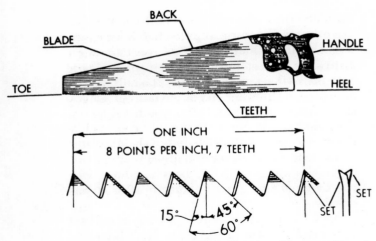

Crosscut saw-teeth are like knife-points. They crumble out the wood between the cuts.

Saws

Crosscut Saw

One of the most delightful experiences in carpentry is to see the ease with which you can slice across even thick pieces of lumber with a sharp crosscut saw. The fact that this tool cuts on both the up stroke and the down stroke also serves to make the job go faster. For most carpenter's work, select an 8- or 9-point saw. These numbers apply to the spacing of the teeth. In this instance it means that there are 8 or 9 teeth to the inch. A saw of this type is fine for general carpentry and will handle nearly any cabinet-making task you want to tackle.

On the other hand, if you're going to do mostly fine work, buy a saw that has 10 points to the inch. You will find this information usually stamped somewhere on the blade.

As for lengths, although they range from 20 to 28 inches, you'll probably find a 26-inch saw the best for all-around work. Incidentally, if portability is your goal, there is also a 12-inch model that is made to fit toolboxes, but it's relatively inconvenient to use because you have to jab at the wood instead of using a nice sweeping motion.

Mark off the guideline along the wood and position the saw against the waste side of the line. Guiding the blade with your knuckle, pull the saw toward you a few times with short strokes, using the back section of the blade, the part nearest the handle. When you have cut a groove deep enough to keep the blade from skittering, start regular strokes, short at first and gradually increasing until you are utilizing the entire length of the blade.

There's no need to bear down on the blade. If the saw-teeth are sharp, they will do most of the work for you. Just maintain an even, steady rhythm. Keep your eye on the cutting-mark, and always saw on the outside of it.

At first, until you get the hang of using the saw, you may have trouble in maintaining a straight cut. This generally means that you are forcing the blade. Until you become a more skilled craftsman, you may want to clamp a straight-edge along the cutting-line as a guide.

Be sure to hold the saw so that it makes a 45-degree angle with the board being cut. The teeth are designed so that they will work most efficiently at this angle. Keep sawing with steady, even strokes until you near the end of the cut. Carefully support the excess wood beyond the cut or else it may break off before you finish the cut.

Make the last few strokes short and light so that you will have as much control as possible.

In the event that you do veer away from the guideline, you can flex the saw-blade very slightly as you continue to saw, and it will gradually return to position. Don't try strong-arm tactics here or you will merely jam the saw-blade in the cut.

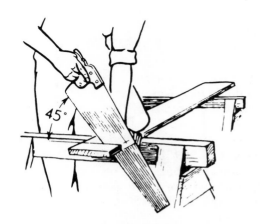

About 45 degrees is the best angle for crosscut sawing.

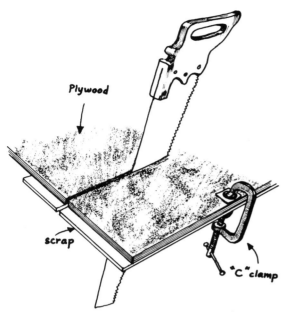

Cut plywood with crosscut saw and back with scrap wood.

Always use a crosscut saw when you are working with plywood, because it will do the job with the least amount of damage to the outer veneer layers. If possible, place another thin board firmly beneath the plywood if you wish to have a perfect cut on both sides.

If for some reason you can only have one saw, make it a crosscut. You can always use it to do work requiring a ripsaw, although progress may be considerably slower. However, do not expect a ripsaw (see below) to do the work of a crosscut. Although it may hack its way through the surface in wood-butcher fashion, the resultant splintering of the wood, especially plywood, will approach criminal proportions.

If you care to spend a little more money in exchange for some additional ease in sawing, or if you're going to be working with wood that is damp or green, you may want to invest in a taper-ground blade. The metal that forms this saw is thinner at the back or straight-edge than along the tooth-section. The metal also tapers so that it is thinner at the hip or far end of the saw than back toward the handle. The purpose is the same: to give you extra clearance and keep the blade from jamming.

Look for a comfortable handle, carefully secured to the saw with three or four fasteners.

Ripsaw

The technique for using this tool is much the same as for crosscutting. However, the angle between the saw and the wood surface should be about 60 degrees in most cases. The only exception would be if you were working on very thin boards. Then keep a 45-degree angle.

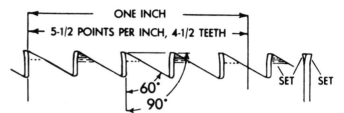

Ripsaw teeth are shaped like chisels.

About 60 degrees is the best angle for ripsawing.

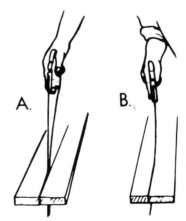

A: If the saw leaves the line, twist the handle slightly, and draw it back to the line.
B: If the saw is not in line with the stock, bend it a little and gradually straighten it.

The starting procedure is a little different, too. Ripsaws are made with finer teeth toward the front end of the blade. The purpose is to make it easier to start a cut. So you will probably wind up with a saw having 5½ teeth to the inch (known as 5½ point).

An indicator of quality is a section at the tip of the blade with more teeth to the inch.

Using only this tip-section of the blade, draw the saw backward several times until you have formed a groove deep enough to guide the blade. Then, working with short strokes still at the tip of the blade, saw gently to deepen the groove. Gradually increase the length of your stroke until you are working with the full sweep of the blade.

Avoid the tendency to jab at the wood with fast, vibrating strokes. It will not complete the job more quickly, and the cut may wander off the marked guideline.

Keyhole Saw

Use a gentle hand with this tool. The fine-tipped blade doesn't have much strength and it has virtually no support. As a result, it's easy to bend and kink it. Work carefully to avoid any flexing on the blade. In case you do bend the blade, you can usually straighten it.

This narrow-blade, pointed-tip saw has been developed for use with a wide variety of blades, each one intended for a specific material, such as wood, plastic, or metal. A "nest" with several different blades can be hooked individually onto the same handle.

Often where a large opening is needed in the middle of a piece of wood, a series of augur-bit holes can be drilled, and the keyhole saw joins them to create the hole of the desired size. In a more limited way, the coping saw can also do this.

Small children often start sawing through small pieces of wood with these light little saws (some are wider than others, like miniature crosscuts). There's an electrical version of this tool called the power-jigsaw that has a fantastic variety of blades to accomplish an unbelievable number of sawing jobs. (See Chapter 5, Power-tools.)

Coping Saw

This light little 6-inch saw with a thin fragile blade is extremely handy for youngsters and amateurs. It has two kinds of blades, both easy to insert. One is for sawing thin pieces of wood, and the other, the hardened tempered-steel blade, can cut through wire and even small pieces of pipe. You may break the blade if you do not keep it tight with the fasteners. However, the blades are inexpensive, and you can buy a dozen or so at a time. The coping saw fits easily into the tool-kit.

A professional degree of skill is needed to make perfect joints in intricate moldings for ceilings and floors. Cutting the true 45-degree angle with a miter is difficult enough for an amateur, but using the coping saw to fit the angles and curves together seems impossible. Most amateurs resort to wood-filler and paint. (See Chapter 6, Finishing Interior Walls, Kitchens, Baths.)

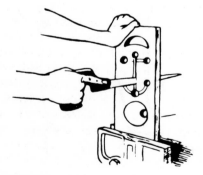

Keyhole or compass saws are used to cut curved or straight-sided holes in areas that can't be reached by other saws.

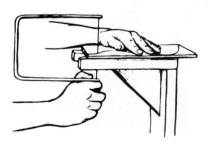

The coping saw is used to cut irregular shapes and intricately curved patterns in thin wood.

Backsaw

Used for precision-cutting, this saw, which looks like a cleaver, is actually very thin, with fine teeth. Normally it is fitted in with a miter box, so the wood can be cut on precise angles, such as 45-degree picture-frame angles. All miter boxes also cut 90-degree angles.

For sawing metal at precise angles, there are miter boxes that will hold a hacksaw in the fixed position necessary.

Miter Box

For cutting lengths of wood (such as moldings and picture frames) at an angle, this guide will help you do a neat and accurate job. It is available in several different forms, from an inexpensive wood-frame saw-guide all the way up to a very fancy metal rig; it's just a matter of selecting the one that suits your purpose and pocketbook. The inexpensive varieties are usable for only a few cuts, such as 90-degree or 45-degree; the higher-priced metal variations can produce an entire range of angled cuts, and have a built-in saw known as a backsaw that will give greater accuracy to the angle of the cut needed.

Hacksaw

This tool is absolutely necessary for cutting metal. Around the house you'll use it for cutting through pipe or slicing through the metal spiral on the outside of BX cable. Select a hacksaw that has two or more blade-positions so that you can shift the blade in the frame and cut up or down, right or left.

The backsaw is a thin crosscut saw with fine teeth, stiffened by a thick back. A popular size is 12 inches with 14 points per inch. It is used for fine, accurate work.

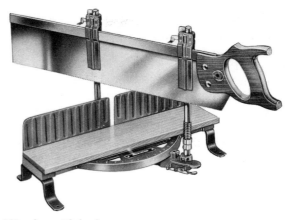

Miter box with backsaw

Hacksaw

Hacksaw blades come with teeth ranging from 14 to 32 per inch. The best for all-around work is the 18-tooth one. Hacksaws are designed with a metal frame that holds the blade under tension. Check the tool in the store to make sure this tension feature is easily adjustable. Buy a few additional blades so that you will have a couple of fine ones and a couple of coarser ones on hand.

Mount the blade so that the teeth point forward. With this tool, you cut on the push stroke. To use it, grasp the handle in one hand and the front corner of the hacksaw in your other hand. Press down lightly as you push forward. Pull the blade up a bit on the return-stroke. If you apply any downward pressure on this back-stroke, you merely wear out the blade without adding progress to the cut.

Make sure that you have matched the blade to the work. The relationship is direct. Use a fine-tooth blade on thin stock, coarse teeth on thick stock. It is important to adjust the angle of the saw to the work. This is especially true if you are cutting thin stock. Always have at least two teeth resting on the material being cut. If you are trimming thin stock, then you may have to hold the hacksaw at a very shallow angle to the surface in order to keep this ratio.

If you happen to break a blade while working and try to resume a cut with a new blade, you're in for a surprise. The odds are good that the new blade will merely jam in the old cut. There's a reason for this. Like wood-cutting saws, the teeth on the hacksaw blade are set; that is, they are bent alternately to one side and then to the other. As you use a blade, this overhang is gradually worn down so the blade along the tooth-section gradually becomes thinner. A new blade that has not gone

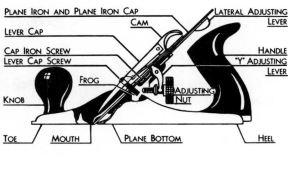

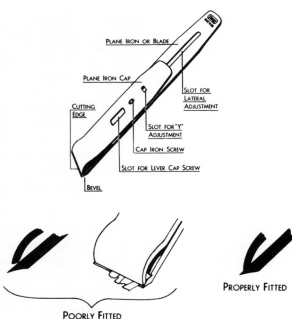

Edge of plane-iron cap must fit to prevent shavings wedging under it, piling up and choking the plane.

through this procedure will have its full thickness, and it will jam. To avoid this, turn the work around and start a new cut from the other side, working toward the old cut.

Wood-plane

Working with a wood-plane can be a very satisfying experience. If the tool is sharp and the wood smooth-grained, you can zip along the surface with very little effort, peeling off great coils of fine shavings. As a matter of fact, this used to be a test given to an apprentice: he had to peel off shavings long enough to reach over his shoulder and down to the ground. If he could accomplish this, it meant he had a sharp, well-adjusted plane and just the right touch for using it.

The *jack-plane,* generally 12 to 15 inches long, can bridge across unevenness in the surface of a board so that it will trim off the high spots without touching the valleys. Incidentally, this tool was once called a jackass-plane, because professional carpenters considered it the workhorse of their array.

If you don't intend to do much cabinet-work, and if sharpening tools is pretty far down on your list of priorities, you might consider investing in a plane that uses the new disposable blades. Perhaps more than any other tool, a plane depends for its smooth action on a very sharp, carefully-honed blade. The disposable type can be replaced when it gets dull, instead of being resharpened.

The secret, if there is one, of using a jack-plane properly is in getting ready. Slicing-tools such as planes and chisels won't do the job if they are not sharp. (For step-by-step advice on sharpening tools, see Chapter 12.)

Although it's hard to go wrong using a plane, since it is probably one of the simplest tools in the entire assortment, it's very important that you spend a little extra time adjusting the blade. First, remove the lever cap. This is the cast-iron piece that fits over the blade or bevel. It has a flip-lever cap or cam at the top to keep it and the blade in position. Notice that the cutting-mechanism is really a two-piece affair. Attached to the blade is another part called an "iron cap," which acts to deflect the shavings.

The iron cap should be positioned ¹/₁₆ inch back of the cutting edge. This adjustment will do for almost all jobs unless you are working with cross-grained or curly wood. In this case, slide it as close to the cutting-edge as possible. Hold the two parts firmly in place and tighten the lever-cap screw that holds them together. Put this assembly back into the plane, slip the lever-cap on top and press down the cam.

Hold the plane upside-down and sight along it. To set the depth of cut, turn the wheel adjusting-nut in and out as you keep your eye on the amount of blade projecting from the plane. There are no hard-and-fast rules, so you'll have to check the adjustment on a piece of scrap-wood.

Planes also have a lateral adjusting-lever that swings from side to side with finger pressure. Sight along the underside of the plane once more as you flip this lever back and forth. Notice that the blade rises up on first one corner and then the other. With this lever you can compensate for any slight diagonal that may have been ground into the blade. Ideally, the same amount of plane-blade should be exposed from one side to the other.

To use a plane, hold it with both hands. Assuming you're right-handed, keep your left hand on the knob as a guide for controlling the direction of the cut, and your right hand on the handle for supplying the force. As you start one pass across the board, press down more on the knob than you do on the handle. Then, as you move across the board, keep full pressure on both knob and handle. As you finish up the stroke, lighten the pressure and lift the plane off the surface. The purpose of this maneuver is to keep the cut flat. Most novice woodworkers have an unfortunate tendency to round the wood by applying too much pressure at the beginning and end of the strokes.

Always plane with the grain of the wood. You can quickly check for this. If the surface has a ridged or pitted look after you make one pass across it, reverse the direction of your stroke. All cutting is done on the forward stroke, so do not drag the plane backwards. Instead, lift it and bring it back into position for the next stroke.

Slip the lever-cap under the lever-cap screw and press down the cam. If the plane-iron is in the correct position, the cam will easily snap in place. If the cam will not snap in place easily, slightly loosen the lever-cap screw. If the plane-iron is not firmly held when the cam is in place, slightly tighten the lever-cap screw.

To adjust for the thickness of the shaving, sight along the bottom of the plane and turn the adjusting nut until the cutting-edge projects about the thickness of a hair.

Knob, lever-cap, and plane-iron cap removed to show the action of the lateral adjusting-lever.

Planing end-grain can be a little tricky; it's very easy to split the wood as you go over the edge of the board. To avoid this, wherever possible, plane from either edge to the center of the wood so the blade never passes over the edge in an outward direction. If you wind up with a slight high spot in the center of the board you can plane this down last.

Another technique is to clamp a piece of scrap-wood against the edge of the board. Set the scrap flush with the end of the board you

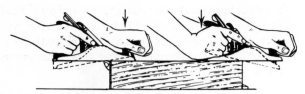

How to use the jack-plane

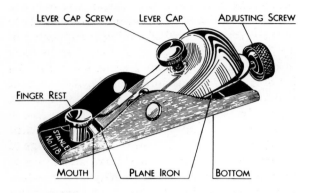

LEVER CAP SCREW   LEVER CAP   ADJUSTING SCREW

FINGER REST

MOUTH   PLANE IRON   BOTTOM

The block-plane has a single plane-iron set at a lower angle than the plane-iron of the smooth plane, enabling it to cut end-grain better than other planes.

are smoothing. You will still split the end of the wood with this technique, but since it's a piece of scrap you'll be battering, it doesn't really matter.

If you have a large amount of material to remove, start work with a coarser adjustment. When you are down close to the line, readjust the plane for a finer cut, and continue to work. To check your progress, place a square or straight-edge across the surface and hold it up to the light. You will be able to spot the places where the edges do not rest firmly against the wood.

Although the plane is adjustable, if you are going to be doing a great deal of rough work such as cleaning up old boards, don't even try to do it with a regular plane. For jobs such as this, you will need a tool called a *scrub-plane*. This is designed specifically to do the rough-tough job of cleaning up old lumber.

The *block-plane* is a stubby one, not commonly used by the householder, but you ought to consider buying one. It's really a clean-up

plane that can safely be used with one hand on the edge of boards — planing inward, without running the risk of beveling the wood.

It can even be used on such small and intricate pieces of wood as the edges of moldings and floorboards.

But it will not make a straight-edge on a long board because of its shortness. It will even cause high and low spots, which the longer jack-plane will not.

Surform Tools

Many of the jobs normally assigned to a plane can be handled perfectly well with one of these new surface-forming tools. Although they are not adjustable, they come in different forms that can be used for shaping, trimming, and forming all sorts of wood-surfaces in addition to plastics and soft metals.

For shaping large, flat surfaces, you can buy a surform tool that looks and works much like a plane. It has a handle at the back for pushing and a knob in the front for guiding. Another variety is patterned after a block-plane. For fast, on-the-job touch-ups, it's hard to beat. A third type looks more like a rasp or file.

To use any of these tools, follow the technique of pushing it forward with one hand on the back handle while you guide the gadget with your other hand on the front knob or surface. All of these tools cut only in the forward direction, so for the return-stroke, lift it off the surface. The one-handled shaver surform, however, has a pulling rather than a

Plane type

Block-plane type

Rasp or file type

pushing motion. Both coarse or fine cutting surfaces can be fitted to the tool.

Surface-forming tools are generally self-cleaning because they have a series of open, mesh-like cutting-edges. The shavings just pass through the blade. Also, because of the multiple cutting-edges, these tools work well on the end-grain of wood. For any application, try to use smooth, even strokes, with light to moderate pressure. There's no need to bear down on the tool. If you do, you'll merely create a series of gouges instead of a smoothly-planed surface.

Check over the wood carefully before you work with any smoothing tool. It takes only one nail to wreck a plane-blade or severely damage a surface-forming tool. This means you'll have to stop work and either resharpen the plane-blade or replace the surface-forming blade. (It doesn't have to be resharpened.) In either event, it's a waste of time.

If you notice that the blade on your surface-

forming tool starts to chatter, it's a tip-off that it's time to replace the blade. If this does not solve the problem, it means you're using incorrect pressure or working against the grain of the wood.

Wood-chisel

In a lot of ways, a chisel is pretty much like a plane. The main difference is that you hold the blade in your hands and use a hammer deftly to make the cut instead of having it supported in a metal plane-body. Also, a chisel can be used with the blade in two positions — with the bevel up and with the bevel down — so that you have twice the possible cutting-actions of a plane. In spite of its versatility, don't use a chisel for a job that you can do more easily with another tool. If you attempt to trim the edge of a board with a chisel, you'll have no chance of keeping the surface smooth. Why bother, when you can handle this task better and more easily with a plane?

A chisel is a superb tool for hollowing out a recess in a board. For example, if you want to mount a hinge-leaf on wood, mark off the position of the hinge, then line up the chisel with the mark at one side, and score the grain with the chisel. (See also Chapter 9, Windows and Outer Doors.) The bevel-part of the chisel-blade should face in toward the hinge and the flat surface should face out away from it. Notice that the first cut will be made perpendicular to the grain of the wood.

Hold the chisel absolutely straight up and down and tap the end of it lightly with a

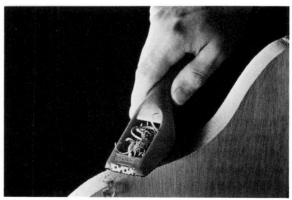

Shaver type

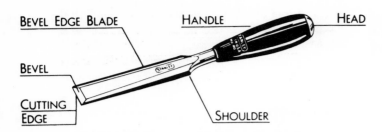

BEVEL EDGE BLADE   HANDLE   HEAD

BEVEL

CUTTING EDGE

SHOULDER

The wood-chisel is controlled with the left hand, pressing firmly on the chisel and the wood. The power is applied with the other hand.

To cut horizontally with the grain, the chisel is held slightly turned to one side and then pushed so the edge slides across the work, or it is moved to the right and left as it is advanced, to give a sliding action to the cutting-edge. This is easier than a straight thrust and leaves a smoother surface on the work. At all times, keep both hands back of the cutting-edge. It is held with the bevel down for a rough cut and with the bevel up for a paring cut.

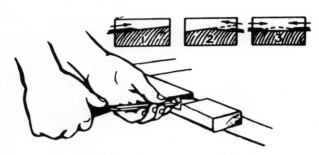

To cut horizontally across the grain to avoid splintering the corners, cut halfway from each edge toward the center. Remove the center-stock last.

To cut a chamfer: hold the chisel inclined to one side parallel to the slope of the chamfer and cut with the grain.

The mallet is safely used on the chisel when the cut is across the grain. With the grain, the mallet is likely to split the wood. The mallet is used to beat out a mortise, and to cut a mortise when the bulk has been bored out, when the wood is hard, and when there is a large amount to be removed.

To cut vertically across the grain, the chisel should be tilted to give a sliding action to the cutting-edge.

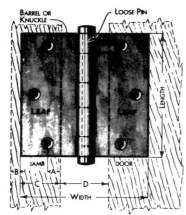

Chiseling gain (or inset) for butt door-hinge
A: Keep this distance sufficient to prevent splitting.
B: Set back far enough to prevent splitting when chiseling.
C: Width of the grain
D: Maximum clearance when door is open

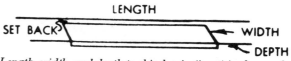

Length, width, and depth to chisel gain (inset) in door and jamb.

Gain scored and ends notched with chisel to aid in removing wood.

Gain (inset) finished, the bottom smoothed by paring with chisel

hammer or mallet. Next, turn the chisel around and line up the blade with the pencil-mark for the other side of the same hinge-leaf. The bevel-side of the chisel again faces in toward the hinge. Tap the handle of the chisel.

Do not follow the same routine along the third marked line. This line runs parallel to the grain of the wood. As a result, it is very easy to split the wood with a mere tap on the chisel-handle. Instead, using the chisel, make a series of parallel cuts or notches across the wood along the line marked for cutting. Then, holding the chisel bevel-side down, either push it with your hand or tap gently with a hammer or mallet to trim out the material between the two side lines of the pocket you're cutting.

As you work, occasionally use one corner of the chisel-blade as a sort of V-shaped knife, with the bevel facing toward the center area. Pull the chisel toward you, guiding it carefully with your fingers gripping near the tip of the chisel. This maneuver trims the line side of a hinge pocket and keeps that line straight.

It's a good idea to practice this maneuver on some scrap-wood first, because the technique requires a bit of skill.

Deeper notches, such as for a mortise, are made by drilling out most of the material inside the outline with a brace-and-bit, and then cleaning up the edges with a chisel, using a paring action. Remember that the bevel-side of the blade always faces toward the waste section of the wood.

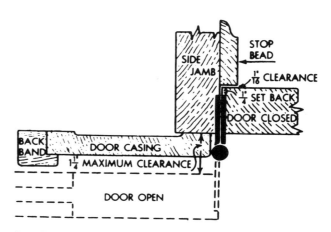

Completed installation of hinge

If you are cutting a notch or a pocket that extends to the edge of the wood, you can use the chisel with the flat-surface down and the beveled-section toward the center of the pocket to clean out excess wood. Work carefully and slowly, using hand-pressure or very light taps with the hammer or mallet. Keep the fingers of one hand just back of the cutting-edge so that you can guide the tool easily.

Usually, for light cuts in soft wood, you can push the chisel forward by hand-pressure alone. For working in hardwood, however, you will have to apply tapping force with a hammer or mallet. Assuming you're right-handed, try to work with your left hand holding and guiding the chisel while you apply the hammer action with your right hand.

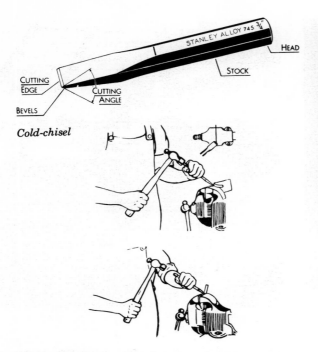

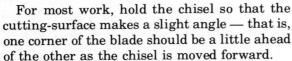

Cold-chisel

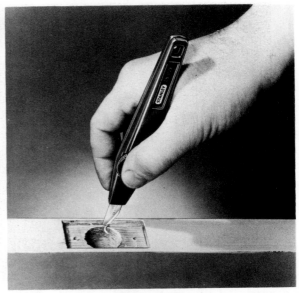

Two types of new pocketknives: midget and retractable (with five blades)

For most work, hold the chisel so that the cutting-surface makes a slight angle — that is, one corner of the blade should be a little ahead of the other as the chisel is moved forward.

Do not under any circumstances try to work with a dull chisel. You will have to apply so much force to make it cut that your control will be practically non-existent. A sharp chisel properly handled will trim off a series of thin shavings, leaving the wood-surface smooth and bright. (For sharpening, see Chapter 12.) Don't chip the edge of a chisel by using it as a screwdriver or wedge, as many amateurs do.

There are, of course, many types of chisels, such as the carving gouge for the dedicated woodworker.

Cold-chisel

This is the toughest hand-cutting tool in common use. It can knock off rusty nuts from bolts, and in a vise, it can be used with some precision.

Hold sheet metal in a vise, and strike the chisel with a hammer so that the excess metal is sheared off along the top of the vise. Or hold a rod, such as a curtain-rod, in the vise and nick it all around so that it can be bent back and forth with pliers to break it.

Pocketknife

Here are two *new* pocketknives — a midget that should do whatever a blade is called on to do, and a sharp retractable trimmer that is as sharp as a utility or carpenter's knife and carries extra blades. It will trim a latch-hole far more neatly than the old-fashioned type.

Bernz Cutter

Not so easy as a tinsnip nor so powerful as a lineman's side-cutting pliers, this pair of shears gives you the power of a utility-knife with better control. In appearance, it seems to be a gun type of tool, although the action is considerably different. By squeezing the "trigger," the tool will make straight or curved cuts through light plywood, house-siding, wire-screening, plastic laminate, roofing-shingles, galvanized metal, hardboard, and a long list of other materials.

Abrasives, Sandpaper

Closed- and open-coat
For most work, you will probably use a material known as closed-coat abrasive, in

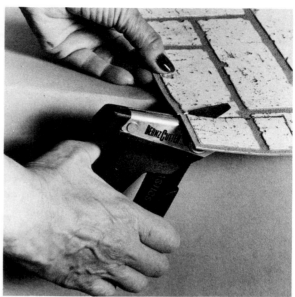

Bernz cutter

which the particles are fairly close together. If you are working on a surface that will clog the abrasive, you should choose open-coat: here the particles are spaced far enough apart so the areas in between don't build up with material.

Grades of abrasives

There's also a whole range of grades, running the gamut from very fine to extra coarse.

Extra coarse: Unless you're sanding away layers of paint, you probably will never use an abrasive this rough.

Coarse: This is a workhorse. Use it for removing material, smoothing out deep scratches, or other heavy jobs.

Medium: This is a good grade for all-around use. It will minimize scratches and prepare the surface for finishing. Use it on walls before you paint.

Fine: Use this for the last sanding of the wood surface before you apply the primer or sealer. You can also use it on metal to remove light rust and imperfections.

Very fine: Use this when you are applying several coats of paint or other finish. After each coat has completely dried, sand it very lightly before applying the next layer — the more coats and sandings (up to six or seven), the slicker the finish.

Other grading-systems: There are a couple of

other grading-systems that you ought to know about before heading for the paint or hardware store. One uses symbols ranging from 4½ (the coarsest grade) to 10/0 (the finest variety).

Another system uses numbers ranging from 12 (representing very coarse) to 600 (very fine). But don't let all this confuse you. You can still get by asking for coarse, medium, fine, etc.

Methods of sanding

If you're going to hand-sand a surface that has been coated with paint or other material that tends to clog sandpaper, use the flint variety. This is cheap and you can throw it away as it becomes ineffective.

If by chance you have a power-sander, use an aluminum oxide abrasive. This works a lot faster and the abrasive lasts considerably longer. If the residue can be flushed away with water, and if the surface can stand liquid, use a variety of abrasives, known as wet-or-dry. However, use them wet — that is, with water. As an overall guide, aluminum oxide paper is suitable for most general jobs. It works quickly and stays sharp. Match the abrasive grade to the job. Here's how the various types stack up.

For cabinet-sanding, be sure you back up the abrasive paper with a firm, flat surface. One inexpensive gadget is a *rubber sanding-block*. This grips a ¼-sheet of paper at two ends and

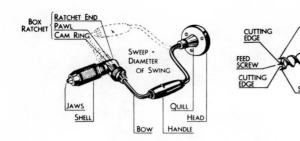

The expansion bit (far right) replaces large bits and can be adjusted for variously sized holes. The most important is probably the doorknob hole, too big for any other bit.

provides proper backing. However, a woodblock will do quite well. Put a straight-edge against the sheet of sandpaper, tear it to size, wrap it around the block, and go to work.

There are a couple of additional tricks that will ease certain types of sanding. For example, if you have to smooth the rungs of a chair or work on legs, tear the sandpaper into long strips. Hold one end in each hand and use it in a back-and-forth motion, much like the motion for polishing shoes. For sanding irregular surfaces, try backing the abrasive paper with a piece of thick foam cut from a kneeling pad (you can buy this item in most hardware and dime stores). (For the two types used in power-sanding, see Chapter 5, Power-tools.)

Brace-and-bit

Because the drill-bits are made with a square-shaped end or shank, it's very easy to fit them into the chuck of the brace. No key or special tool is needed. Merely open the jaws wide enough to admit the bit and insert it as far as it will go. Tighten the chuck, checking to

make certain that the bit is straight, well-centered, and firmly-gripped.

The proper use of this tool calls for firm, even pressure — never brute strength. If the drill-bit is sharp, and if the threads on the end of it are in good condition, this combination will do most of the work for you. The screw-threads will pull the bit into the wood while the cutting-edges will trim away at a satisfying rate.

The tool is used with a simple crank action. If you have lots of room, you can rotate the U-shaped handle round and round in a circle. However, space may be a problem. When you are boring a hole close to a wall and therefore can't get a full swing of the handle, bring the ratchet adjustment of the brace into play. By setting this feature, you can make a partial swing of the handle and then ratchet back to the starting point for another arc. Even though you may have to work in small segments, you will be able to continue the drilling.

Take special pains when the drill-bit reaches the point where it is almost through the wood. If you continue drilling in the same manner,

To operate the ratchet, turn the cam-ring. Turning the cam-ring to the right will allow the bit to turn right and give ratchet action when the handle is turned left. Turn the cam-ring left to reverse the action.

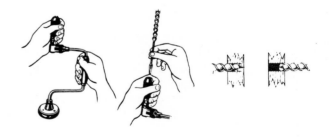

Bit fits into chuck without key. When boring holes, stop drill when tip just projects through wood and resume boring from other side.

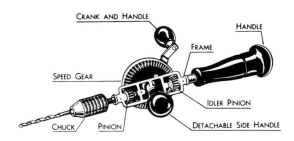

CRANK AND HANDLE
HANDLE
FRAME
SPEED GEAR
IDLER PINION
CHUCK PINION
DETACHABLE SIDE HANDLE

Rotary hand-drill

the bit will splinter the wood on the other side. Stop work when the point of the drill-bit barely projects through the wood. Turn the piece over and finish drilling the hole from the other side. With this maneuver, you will wind up with a smooth, even cut.

However, if you cannot follow this procedure, clamp a piece of scrap-wood in back of the board you are drilling. Bore the hole all the way through the lumber and into the scrap-wood. The purpose is the same: to keep the wood from splintering on the far side.

For general carpentry, the best all-around bit is a type identified as solid-center, single-twist, double-spur-and-cutter with coarse-thread screw-tip. What does all this mean? Here's a fast rundown on the specifications.

The double-spur-and-cutter bit has a solid center for strength. The spiral section that removes the chips pulls the cuttings toward the solid center and then delivers them easily to the surface so they don't jam in the hole. "Double-spur-and-cutter" means that the business-end bores clean with a minimum of effort. A coarse single-thread screw and tip pulls the

bit into the work to ease the wear and tear on your right arm.

Be very careful when working with old wood that may contain nails or other metal fragments. Although drill-bits can be sharpened (see Chapter 12), this is usually a job for the expert or experienced tool-sharpener. Your best course is to protect the cutting-edges so you'll get long and useful service before the tools have to be resharpened.

Doweling

There's a special tool to drill true holes called a doweling-jig. Fitting wood-parts together with dowels has to be done with care, according to size, using a hand-drill, a brace-and-bit, or, or course, an electric-drill.

Rotary Hand-drill

The rotary drill looks like an eggbeater with a chuck at one end. Select one that has a holding handle on the side opposite the rotary gear. If you are going to work in hardwood, some-

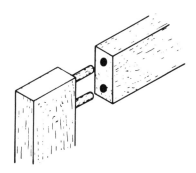

Doweled corner–joint

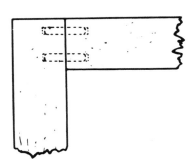

Doweled corner–joint

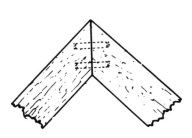

Doweled miter–joint

To insert the drill-point into the chuck, push the chucksleeve forward. Insert the drill-point and turn it until you feel it is seated. Release the chuck-sleeve.

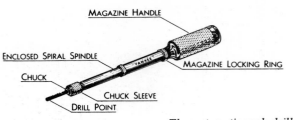

MAGAZINE HANDLE
ENCLOSED SPIRAL SPINDLE
CHUCK
MAGAZINE LOCKING RING
CHUCK SLEEVE
DRILL POINT

The automatic push-drill.

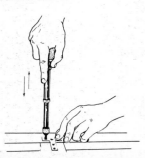

The return-spring reverses the drill-point, clearing away the chips. The automatic push-drill is especially useful in awkward or close places.

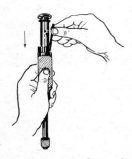

Draw the magazine handle down and turn it to select the desired-size drill-point.

times it is useful to push against the end of the drill with your stomach while you guide the tool with the side-handle.

Like a bit-brace, the rotary drill has a chuck that is opened and tightened by hand. No tools are needed. Don't plan on drilling holes any larger than ¼ inch with this tool. The average "eggbeater" type is geared for boring holes up to this size but is not equipped for anything bigger.

Of course, there is a jumbo version of the rotary drill, known as a breast-drill, that will take considerably larger bits. However, for anything beyond ¼ inch, or for working in very hard materials, you'll probably want to switch to a hand electric-drill or to a brace-and-bit.

For light-duty work, hold the tool with one hand on the handle while you turn the crank with the other. For horizontal holes, or in areas where you can press against the end of the handle with your stomach, you can get a little additional force by holding onto the sidehandle with one hand while you turn the crank with the other.

Push-drill

The push-drill is an alternate tool to the rotary drill. A handy tool, it is intended for very light work only, and its usefulness is limited to soft materials. Drill-bits for the push-drill are considerably different from those for other hole-boring tools. So is the chuck of the tool. Generally, it's a spring-loaded affair; you pull up or down on the chuck to release the clutching mechanism. Insert the drill-bit, turning it slightly until it "seats" properly. Then release the chuck.

Push-drills operate with a retractable action. Use one or both hands to push the tool in a downward motion. This will make the drill-bit revolve and bite into the wood. As you release the pressure, the retractable spring-action will bring the tool back to starting position for the next stroke. This sounds much more cumbersome than it really is. In use, the motion is a rapid in-and-out jiggling movement.

For the most part, you will probably use this tool to make starting-holes for small screws,

 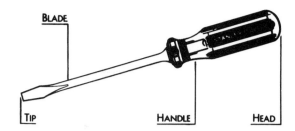

Select a screwdriver fitted to the screw-slot and not wider than the screw-head. Three or four screwdrivers will serve. If the tip is too wide, it will scar the wood around the screwhead. If the screwdriver is not held in line with the screw, it will slip out of the slot and mar both the screw and the work.

pilot-holes for nails so they won't split the wood, and guide-holes for small fixtures such as cup-hooks.

Be careful not to put too much pressure on the drill-bit; because they are fairly small, it is relatively easy to snap them. Also, if you get careless, you may bend the shank-section of the bit. When this happens, it will wobble. Don't even try to straighten the bit. Discard it, buy a replacement, and be more careful next time.

When you have drilled to the bottom of a hole, don't remove the bit by tugging on it. Instead keep rotating the bit as you pull backward on the drill.

Some amateur carpenters favor a multidrill-screwdriver gadget. It often has a compartment in the handle with various sizes of small drill-heads and screwdriver-heads that fit into the chuck of the tool.

Screwdrivers

The screwdriver isn't nearly as simple as it seems: it's important that the tip of the blade fit the slot of a screw. It should be the same shape, width, and thickness. If the blade is too wide and overhangs the side of the screw, it will chew up the wood during the last turn or so. If the blade is too narrow, you won't get enough leverage to turn the screw properly; also, you will batter either the screw or the screwdriver. The tip of the screwdriver should fit down to the bottom of the screw-slot and should be designed to fit the particular screw-head it's been teamed up with.

If you have carefully matched the tip of the blade to the slot in the screw, you have con-

Use the longest screwdriver convenient for the work. More power can be applied to a long screwdriver than to a short one, with less danger of its slipping out of the slot. Hold the handle firmly in the palm of the right hand with the thumb and forefinger grasping the handle. With the left hand, steady the tip and keep it pressed into the slot. If no hole is bored for the screw, the wood will often split or the screw twist off. If a screw turns too hard, back it out and enlarge the hole. A little soap on the threads of the screw makes it easier to drive.

quered most of the job. The rest is automatic. If the blade has a tendency to slip out of the screw-slot, even though it appears to be a good fit, try rubbing the tip of the screwdriver with a bit of chalk. This sometimes adds enough friction to hold the tool in position.

To avoid splitting the wood with a screw, sink pilot-holes for both the threaded section and the smooth section of the screw with a counter-sink drill.

It's a good idea to select the larger-size screwdrivers with a square shank; then, if you are turning large screws or working with very hard wood, you can hook a wrench onto the shank to give you some additional leverage. Don't buy stubby screwdrivers until you really need them for tight spots. They're harder to use and seem to waste some of the energy you put into them. For some reason, a screwdriver with a longer blade is easier to turn and handle. The 6-inch length is probably easiest for most all-around work.

If the screw binds in the hole and becomes hard to turn, rub the threads across a bar of soap. Then, when you turn the screw in place, the soap will act as a lubricant to make the job a great deal easier.

If you are working with small screws in soft wood, there is probably no need to drill guide-holes. Instead, use an awl to form a starting-hole by pressing it into place with your hand.

Unless you are used to fixing watches with your hands, you are probably as fumble-fingered as the rest of us. When trying to get a screw started in cramped quarters, you may lose it. For this contingency, there is an ingenious device, the screw-starter, that has a tiny lock on the end that will hold the screw and get it started. It also lifts out-of-the-way screws that have loosened or have been unscrewed. And if you drop the screw anyway, it has a magnet at the end of the handle to reach it.

There is another model of the screw-starter for Phillips screw-heads.

Push and Ratchet Screwdriver

Some amateur carpenters prefer the push screwdriver. It takes the place of a set of screwdrivers, and it is retractable: the blade will turn a screw as you press the handle down, and will return to normal position as soon as you withdraw the blade from the slot. The ratchet can also be set in a fixed position to screw or unscrew.

Similar to the push-drill, although it's considerably longer and the internal leverage is more rugged, this tool will drive a screw home with satisfying speed. Instead of turning, as you do the regular screwdriver, you merely push. However, it does take a few practice sessions to acquire the knack of using this tool easily. The problem is one of control. It's very easy for the screwdriver-bit to slip out of the screw-slot while you're turning it, unless you steady it by holding the chuck-sleeve in the left hand. Of course, there's one very obvious alternative: use Phillips screwdriver bits whenever possible. This hand screwdriver can be converted to a drill, making a push-drill unnecessary in your arsenal of tools. It will operate a counter-sink drill.

Clamps

Until recently, the old-fashioned wooden clamps with a turn-screw at each end were standard with everyone from the cabinet-maker on down. Large and awkward, wooden clamps were resilient and could cope with uneven surfaces, especially furniture-parts.

Here are two metal clamps, recently available, that can do small jobs more efficiently. The spring clamp, a sort of glorified

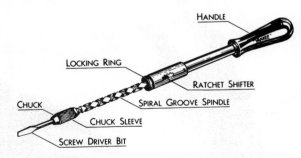

Spiral ratchet screwdriver: to insert the screwdriver-bit into the chuck, place the ratchet shifter on the center position. Pull the chuck-sleeve down. Insert the bit. Turn the bit until you feel it is seated. Release the chuck sleeve.

Spring-clamp

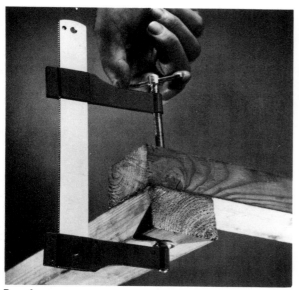

Bar-clamp

Adjustable wrench and pump-type multi-pliers

clothespin, comes in sizes up to a 3-inch opening that is perfect for picture-frames, loose fixtures, and small boards. Plastic grips prevent marring.

The steel-bar clamp opens to 6 inches and can handle lumber up to that width for gluing and screwing. These two clamps should take care of every household need except re-gluing chair-rungs. For this, a piece of rope or a belt will do, though there are special canvas strips with fasteners available at the hardware store if you want to do it the professional way.

Pliers and Wrenches

Pliers and wrenches have been invented for every imaginable purpose. The names can be confusing. The multi-pliers (or pump wrench) shown above are nothing like the multi-purpose pliers shown below, the latter being chiefly a high-grade cutting-tool for wires and bolts. The multi-pliers are mainly for gripping and have serrated jaws for holding round objects, such as pipe from 1¼ inch to 3¼ inch. Instead of having only two positions as in a

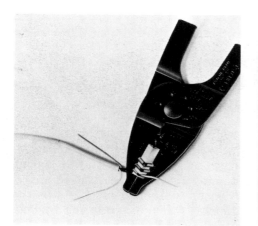
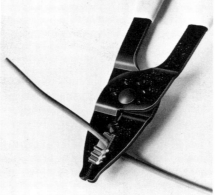

Multi-purpose pliers cuts electrical wire, strips insulation, and cuts bolts and screws

standard slipjoint pliers, this tool may have four or more different settings to grasp objects of various diameters. One joint permits grabbing small objects; by jiggling a pivot, you can open it out to grab larger nuts and bolts.

A pipe wrench is probably the most useful wrench you can have in the house.

The needle-nose pliers are useful for removing finishing-nails without wrecking the finish.

Perhaps half the jobs accomplished by wrenches around the house involve two, not one, wrench. To tighten a nut and bolt, you need a nut-wrench at one end and an adjustable-wrench at the other. Using pliers on a nut, bolt, or pipe may result in chewing them up. In the illustration on page 99, an adjustable wrench is used in combination with pump-type multi-pliers to accomplish a complicated plumbing job.

Screwdriver and nut-driver set

Socket or Nut-driver Wrenches

Once considered the exclusive province of professional mechanics, this tool's usefulness is being discovered by more and more homeowners. It can be set for tightening both square and hexagonal nuts onto their bolts.

Increasingly, amateurs are buying sets of nut-driver wrenches instead of the old-fashioned open-end or box wrenches. (See Chapter 4.) One "journeyman" set includes sockets for both square and hexagonal nuts, as well as screwdriver-heads, both standard and Phillips.

Each nut-driver is designed to fit one specific size of nut or bolt. As a result, there is virtually no chance of slippage (as is the case with some adjustable wrenches as well as pliers).

In some instances, sockets are available individually so that you can expand your collection for such special purposes as changing spark-plugs.

There are three sizes of nut-driver handles, and each one has a range of sockets. For light work, a ¼-inch size will tackle a wide variety of tasks. If you intend to do mostly heavy-duty jobs, however, you will be better off selecting the ½-inch size together with the sockets

designed to fit the ratchet type. For all-around work, there's an intermediate ⅜-inch size.

A ratchet-handle gives you a very rapid action by a mere back-and-forth flip of your wrist. Contrast this with the laborious one-turn-at-a-time tightening procedure that you have to follow with a standard wrench and you will quickly see the advantages.

Using a very ingenious system of telescoping spring-loaded sleeves, one gadget — the adjustable nut-driver — will turn a wide variety of hexagonal nuts. No adjustments are necessary. Merely slip the tool in position over the nut, and the proper sleeve will grip the surface while you tighten.

Measuring and Marking Tools

With the price of lumber and plywood going through the ceiling, there is one old-time carpenter's adage that applies even more today: "Measure twice, cut once."

If you want to put this advice into use, you should acquaint yourself with the various measuring and marking tools used in carpentry. Also, take a little bit of extra time when measuring to make certain you are doing the job with the greatest accuracy.

Six-foot Zig-Zag Rule

This is the familiar spring-joint folding rule that flips out to become a 6-foot-long measuring device. Although at first glance it seems quite simple, there are some very interesting calibrations worked into it. For example, notice that the first section or leg of the rule is shorter than the others by exactly two inches. If you leave the rule folded and allow this shorter segment to extend over the end of the work, you'll have a precise 2-inch marking-guide. Now open up this first segment. Notice that it overhangs the rest of the rule by precisely 4 inches. You now have a handy marking-device for 4 inches.

Hold the rule closed, and open up one segment at the other end to have a 6-inch marking-gauge. Open up one more leg on the side, and you have a 12-inch marking-gauge. The entire rule continues on in this fashion. Because of the way opposite ends of the rule are constructed, and because of the precise dimension of the body of the rule itself, you wind up with a whole series of ready-made marking-gauges in a great many commonly needed increments.

An even more refined version of the zig-zag has a thin extension in the first fold. By pulling this out, you can measure the inside of narrow pipe, a pipe-collar, or a narrow space between boards.

Flexible Tape

Although it's a lot more compact, this tool — 6 feet to 12 feet — will do many of the same tasks as a zig-zag rule. Notice that the case itself can be used as part of the measuring system. Most tapes are made to roll up into a housing that is an exact measurement (usually 2 inches). This comes in especially handy when you are making an inside measurement. You simply place the case against one side wall and extend the tape horizontally until it hits the opposite side wall. The amount of the exposed tape, plus the width of the case, gives you the exact inside measurement. If your tape has a locking-device, this makes the work even easier. Instead of having to read it in a cramped space, you can merely extend the tape and then lock it in position. It will stay at this spot while you take the tape out to where you can take a good and accurate look at it.

Make sure the tape has a sturdy hook at the end designed to hold the tape in place at the edge of a board. Don't be upset if this hook appears to be a trifle loose. It's meant to be. Because of this feature, you can hook it on the outside of a board to take that overall measurement, or you can poke the end of the tape into a corner and still get an accurate reading.

The better varieties of steel tapes have some sort of plastic-finish bonded to the metal to preserve the markings.

A steel tape has a spring device to retract the tape into its case; don't snap it back roughly or crookedly. You may derange the spring and have to take it apart to fix it. The 50-foot and 100-foot steel tapes should have a crank handle on the side like the long non-metallic ones, because the spring-action may not retract the tape automatically after long use.

Try Square

This is a simple basic tool that gauges 90-degree angles from all points on a board. Many prefer this tool to the combination

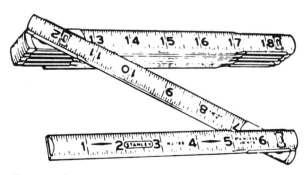

Zig-zag rule

The 1-inch steel tape will extend vertically without support.

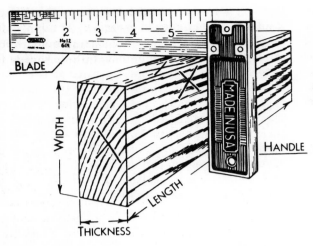

Hold the handle of the try square tight against the board when testing ends and edges, or when scribing lines to make cuts.

Combination-square with sliding level

Carpenter's square

square, which has more built-in features.

Combination Square

As a measuring and marking tool, this 12-inch gadget probably has no equal. It serves many purposes. The blade can slip out of the handle so you can use it as a flat ruler or a straight-edge. Because of the built-in glass bubble tubes, a combination square serves as a fine level for checking both horizontal and vertical surfaces. Because you can slide the blade into various positions, you can wind up with a right-angle device for checking inside square corners as well as outside angles. The same adjustable-blade feature gives you an infinitely variable marking-gauge. Quite handy, if you want to scribe a line down a run of boards.

Most combination squares also have a tiny scriber fitted into the handle. Old-time carpenters swear by these. They claim, and rightfully so, that the fine mark made by the point of a scriber is much more accurate than a pencil line (which is quite a bit broader).

Carpenter's and Homeowner's Square

There are various versions of this tool with different names, and they all look more or less alike: homeowner's square, rafter square, etc. The difference is in the types of markings on the blades and also in the information that's actually engraved into the metal.

Most home-handymen settle for a framing-square, believing it is the most useful model. They are available in several different sizes, the most common of which is 24 by 16 inches.

In using a square, hold the longer side in your left hand and the shorter portion (it's called the tongue) in your right hand. The heel or right angle points away from the body. In this position, the side that is up is the face of the square. The reverse side is called the back of the square.

In using a square to mark a large area, the long side or blade should be held along the edge of the panel, with the tongue across the face of it. Then you draw marking-lines using the tongue as a guide. Many amateurs do not hold the long side firmly against the side of the panel or board, and so draw a line with the tongue that is less than 90 degrees.

All the scales and tables marked off on the square can be confusing at first glance. There are inches and graduations of inches on all edges of the square. But there are also other tables on the carpenter's square that can be most useful to the homeowner, especially if he has the booklet of instructions given with each tool to illustrate the tables.

Let's take these one at a time.

1. The Essex or lumber scale is used to calculate the number of board-feet in a piece of lumber. (See Chapter 11.) This table can save you a great deal of time when estimating lumber requirements for a specific job.
2. Squaring a foundation, especially for an addition to a house: the formula 6 feet–8 feet–10 feet is used to determine whether the foundation is kept square. (See illustration.)
3. Markings for estimating the amount of shingles needed for roof and sides of a house.
4. Formula for determining pilot-holes for different-size screws and drill sizes for them.
5. Points for figuring the number of nails by size (common and finish) per pound.
6. Conversion of measurements from inches to meters.
7. Aids for determining the distance between rafters and studs according to their sizes and other building estimates. mates.

All-in-one Measuring Tool

It scribes circles, marks angle-cuts, checks squareness, and checks plumb and level. It also determines nail, screw, and dowel sizes. It is part combination square, part level, part marking-gauge, part beam-compass, and part protractor. If space is a problem, and if you're tired of looking around for individual tools for each of these jobs, this combination may very well answer your needs.

Wing-dividers

Wing-dividers are used for installing wallboard in uneven corners or along fireplaces (see illustration, Chapter 6, page 30), or anywhere it is necessary to follow an uneven line that has to be matched perfectly. Wing-dividers are also used to mark off evenly divided spaces, such as in measuring a board for beveling or doweling or dovetailing boards in making drawer-joints.

Plumb-bob and Chalk-line Reel

In the illustration on page 104 showing how a carpenter's (or homemaker's) square can serve to determine a foundation, the strings that are maneuvered to form a 90-degree angle are usually weighted with plumb-bobs, almost identical in appearance with the chalk-line reel.

Plumb-bobs are weights which are hung on strings to determine if a wall or structure is perpendicular.

The chalk-line reel (see Chapter 4, page 29) can be hung in place of a plumb-bob; and, because it contains a reel of string inside, it can be used as a foundation-guide in place of the plumb-bob. It is used for marking straight lines on doors, windows, floors, or other clean, hard surfaces. The string comes out coated with chalk and, when snapped taut, makes a straight line on the surface beneath. The carpenter's saying is, "Use the chalk-string first, nail later."

Awl

Among its many jobs, this "ice pick" sticks into wood and can be used to mark and hold measuring-devices. It indents holes for starting nails and screws, anchors taut string-lines on stakes to level foundations, floors, and decks, and spikes down chalk-strings to mark straight lines for sawing boards or erecting walls.

Levels

A level is also known as a *spirit level*, perhaps because the little glass or plastic bubble tubes that are set into the body are partly filled with alcohol. When the air-bubble settles between two marked lines on the tube, the surface you are checking is level or plumb. Most levels have at least two tubes, one for horizontal leveling and the other for insuring

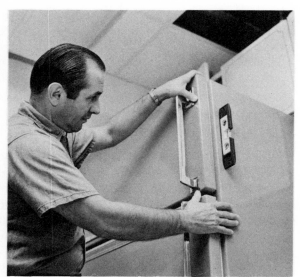

Magnetic torpedo level

Magnetic carpenter's level

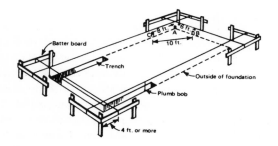

that a vertical board or structure is 90 degrees. Some levels have an additional tube so that you can also check a 45-degree angle, usually for measuring braces.

Torpedo Level

The little 6-inch torpedo level is useful in a hundred ways around the house to indicate whether a surface is level. Some torpedo levels have the bubble that indicates both 90 degrees and 45 degrees. The magnetic one is a bit larger, and it frees the hands by attaching itself to metal, such as a refrigerator or cabinet.

Carpenter's Level

This varies from 2 to 4 feet in length and is necessary for all large construction jobs, to level newly-installed floors, walls, windows, decks and such.

Using a carpenter's level is absolutely necessary and is simplicity itself. Merely tilt it up and down until the air-bubble comes to rest between the marks in the proper tube. If you are leveling a long piece of wood, rest the level on top and jockey both the timber and the level until the bubble comes to rest at the proper point, the mid-point. Your carpenter's level should, of course, have 90-degree verticals as well as 45-degree angles.

Line Level

A miniature version of the carpenter's level, this is used for totally different purposes. About the size of an old-fashioned fountain-pen, the gadget has only one bubble tube built into it, and it has a loop or hook fastened to either end. The tool is hooked over a taut string or a *plumb-line*. It is handy for checking the level of two widely separated points before a board is put in place. You will probably use this device for aligning and leveling a series of posts for patio supports, a porch, a floor, or a roof-line.

In constructing a foundation or floor or any level surface, the plumb-line, plumb-bob, and line level are all used to assure a level surface.

11
Materials

It can be very confusing the first time you walk into a lumberyard. You'll see stacks of hardware and wood inside and outside, and the man behind the counter will ask you questions to which you may not have the vaguest answers. It is confusing but actually not all that complex. After reading this book, you will be astonished to recognize in the lumber store and yard many things you never noticed before, though they were always right in front of you. Even a little knowledge can go a long way, and you will soon begin to feel like an expert. Here's a quick rundown on the basic facts about lumber.

Lumber

Woods are divided into two general categories — hardwoods and soft woods. These designations refer to the kind of trees the wood comes from. Hardwoods come from broad-leafed trees, while soft woods come from evergreens. However, although most hardwoods are harder than soft woods, this is not always true. For example, Douglas fir, although called a soft wood, is a lot tougher than a hardwood like Philippine mahogany. To cap the confusion, the soft balsa wood that kids use to build model airplanes is technically called a hardwood.

If you are looking for a general guide, think in terms of the finished use. Cabinet-woods such as walnut, mahogany, and oak are generally used for making furniture or hardwood flooring. Unless you get into this type of work, you will be mostly concerned with the so-called soft woods for the various jobs that you tackle about the house.

Source is another factor. Although you may be totally sold on redwood, you will be able to obtain it at reasonably low cost only in the Northwest. Redwood is quite common there, but it's relatively rare in the East. The reason for the increased cost is shipping. By the same token, pine is a wood vastly more common in the South and Southeast. When you make an actual visit to the lumberyard, these distinctions become academic. Unless you're prepared to do some shopping around, you will probably settle for the material they have right there. However, the charts that follow will probably be of some help.

Board Dimensions

You may be billed by your lumberyard for board-feet rather than the number of boards you ordered. On the carpenter's square that is so essential for squaring and measuring larger construction jobs, the reverse side (which carries the manufacturer's name in the corner) has a scale called the Essex board measure table, which is what professional carpenters use to measure board-feet in ordering lumber. Most amateurs, however, find they cannot use this to order lumber because it's somewhat complicated. At best, one should remember to order 10 percent more board-lumber than the job calls for, to allow for wastage, such as short ends. "Board-feet" are estimated by cubic inches, and price is determined on this basis. It is enough for the amateur to ask the price of boards by the foot, and to know the lengths in which they can be obtained and most usefully cut on the job.

Grade of Lumber

Whenever you buy wood, make certain it is well-seasoned and dry, or it will shrink after you have constructed with it. Your only guide is the integrity of the place where you buy the wood. For this reason, it's a good idea to deal with a local source who depends for his livelihood on further business from you.

Grades of Lumber of All Types:

1 & 2 Clear: Used for furniture and other projects demanding the finest quality. Almost entirely free of defects.

Grade C: This will have minor blemishes on one side, but none on the other.

Grade D: Possible to use with a natural finish, it is serviceable wood of the lowest grade.

Number 1: Sound but with knots; most useful for painted surfaces.

Number 2: May be used for rugged-looking flooring, but has sizable knots.

Number 3: Rough lumber, with some sap; not for living quarters.

Number 4: Poor quality though sturdy, suitable for making concrete forms, etc.

Number 5: Crating material.

Decide exactly what grade of lumber you really need for the specific project you are going to tackle. Certainly first-grade lumber is a pure delight to work with; it's almost entirely free of blemishes, and it has been carefully processed and stored. However, this type of lumber is not necessary for all types of construction. For example, for the inside studs of a new wall, you do not have to go to the expense. Perhaps you can get by with C-grade.

Be sure to seek advice from the man behind the counter. Sometimes a lumberyard may be stuck with odd lots of lumber it's having trouble unloading. If you fill the salesman in on the type of project you're tackling, there's a chance he may have "orphans" like this that are perfectly suitable for your task. Happily, the price may reflect his desire to get rid of this material. But you don't want warped wood for a floor or a deck, and you will have to insist on returning unusable pieces.

Wood Terms

Although the terminology varies around the country, there are some fairly well established names for the various types of lumber. Wood that is less than 2 inches thick is generally referred to as a "board." Thicker pieces of wood are referred to as "dimensional lumber." "Posts" are square pieces of wood — 2x2, 4x4, etc. Narrow pieces of wood are sometimes called "strips." Dimensional lumber used for framing-supports inside house-walls (2x3, 2x4, 2x6, etc.) are referred to as "studs." Really big hunks of wood are called "timbers."

Plywood

This sandwich-type of material is made of several thin layers of wood glued together. This construction gives the material fantastic strength in all directions. By contrast, solid-wood has strength when the force is perpendicular to the grain. However, it splits quite easily along the grain. For its weight, plywood is probably one of the strongest building materials you can find.

Most of the strength of a plywood sheet is on the face or back. The thin edges, because of the

An elaborate room, combining plywood paneling and boards as flooring, planter, and trim. For such a room, a careful plan of the amount of wood of each kind must be worked out before ordering.

sandwich-type of construction, will not hold nails, screws, or other fasteners with any degree of strength.

Sizes

Plywood is a modular material: it is not cut directly from a tree, so few of nature's restrictions apply. The common-size panel is 4x8 feet. Sizes ranging from 36 to 60 inches wide are supposed to be available, but don't expect to find them in stock in every lumberyard. By the same token, you can buy 4-foot plywood panels in lengths ranging all the way up to 12 feet, although the yard may have to order it specifically for you, and the wait could be considerable.

Types

The grades, types, and variations in which plywood is available make quite a list. Usually, for most home-building and repair projects, it is necessary to know about only a few specific types. Thickness is another variation. Generally the range includes ¼, ⅜, and ½ inch for interior work, and ⅝, ¾, ⅞, 1, and 1⅛ inches for outer walls and roofs. Admittedly, some of these are little more than catalog listings. Most lumberyards stock ¼-, ½-, and ¾-inch-thick material, to satisfy the demand for paneling or construction work. Cheaper grades are available for subflooring in widths of ¼ inch and ⅜ inch, and for walls and roofing in widths of ¾ inch to 1 inch. The difference in exterior-grade and interior-grade plywood is primarily in the glue that bonds the layers together. In plywood intended for exterior use, a waterproof glue is used. The layers of the material meant for use inside the house would separate under moist conditions.

Hard and Soft Plywood

Like lumber, plywood comes in two main categories. The hardwood variety is used as an interior wall-finish (wall-paneling) in such fine cabinet-woods as walnut, teak, mahogany, birch, and cherry. This material is also excellent for cabinet- and furniture-making.

Soft-wood plywood, chiefly a construction material, is usually fir, although you may find other finer-grade soft woods such as Philippine mahogany, cedar, and pine, which together make up more than half of all the plywood sold. The hard or soft plywood material refers, of course, only to the *veneer* that is used on the face of the sheet. It has nothing to do with the material forming the layers inside. And the veneer has nothing to do with quality: it may be ¼-inch full of knotholes or the finest teak or mahogany.

Grades

Like lumber, plywood ranges from perfect to much less so. The variations, of course, are in the appearance of the surface veneer. The designations are different for hardwood and soft-wood plywood. In hardwood, the veneer range goes like this: No. 1 is very expensive, absolutely perfect. Generally, a sheet of this type, such as teakwood, must be specially ordered. It is used only for the most deluxe jobs. In No. 2, the matching of veneers is not quite as precise, although you may not notice the difference. No. 3 is perfectly serviceable if you intend to paint the wood.

Here's how the different grades of less-expensive soft plywood shape up:

Grade N is top of the heap. This designation will have no defects at all and the veneers will be all hardwood or all sap-wood. If you insist on a perfect transparent finish (such as lacquer), this is your best choice, although you will certainly pay for the luxury. Panels of matching grain are the most difficult to obtain, and you or an architect will have to make sure of a satisfactory result.

In grade A, the surface may have some small matching veneer patches over the original knot-holes, but for the most part they will be virtually imperceptible. Because of this, you can apply a clear or natural finish to the surface as well as paint it.

In grade B, the patchwork is more crude and obvious, with plugs of veneer over the tight knot-holes. But the surface will be smooth enough to take a decent paint-finish.

In grade C, the knot-holes are larger, the plywood is still cheaper, and the surface may include some small splits running along the grain of the veneer. A few minor repairs with wood-filler may be necessary before you can get a smooth painted finish.

A grade known as C-plugged is at the lower end of the C-grade. Splits may be up to ⅛ inch wide, and knot-holes may be as large as ½ inch wide and an inch or two long. Considerable patching is necessary if you intend to use this for relatively fine work, and it has to be painted to hide the patches.

Grade D is really a utility material. It can have knot-holes as large as 3 inches in width, plus a considerable sprinkling of splits. You will see this heavy plywood used in construction work, for concrete forms or for roof construction that will be covered with shingles.

Plywood is also designated as being good on

one side or on both sides. If you are involved in a project such as wall-board, where only one side of the sheet will show, it's foolish to spend the money on plywood that is good on both sides.

Special Finishes

For a premium price, you can buy plywood that has already been worked into an interesting assortment of surface finishes or textures. For example, you can buy material that has been sanded to a smooth finish or has been impregnated with a special resin so that it will accept paint for a slick finish. You can also buy comparatively inexpensive plywood panels with a series of grooves that simulate vertical planking.

Pre-finished plywood generally consists of a few layers of lacquer and wax applied right at the factory. It's well worth the extra cost. You can buy plywood in various colors and patterns as well as in all sorts of textures.

Forage through the stock and the catalog sheets at your local lumberyard or building-supply company. The variety will seem infinite.

There is another type that you should know about. Material is now available with a vinyl film bonded onto the surface. This may be clear, but it may also be imprinted to simulate marble, exotic woods, or some other texture.

As a guide to quality, look for a stamping with the letters DFPA along the back or along the edges of the sheet. This stands for Department for Product Approval and indicates that the material meets the specifications of the American Plywood Association.

Other Variations

You can also buy a similar material known as *core-wood*, which can be spotted quite easily because the middle layer is extra thick. This middle layer constitutes the bulk of the sheet, with the thin veneer layer on either side completing the sandwich. It is used principally for table-tops or similar heavy-duty construction.

Particle-board (some people refer to it as chip-wood) has a core made up of chopped-wood particles bonded together with resin. It has a thin veneer on either side to complete the sandwich. However, particle-board is also available without the veneer ply. Suitable for many of the same interior (but not decorative) purposes as plywood, it is not as strong, and it generally costs less.

Hardboard is a single-layer material, not a veneer sandwich like plywood. It is made by squeezing a wood-pulp mixture into sheets under intense heat and pressure. There are two main varieties of hardboard — tempered and untempered. You will probably use the untempered variety for most jobs about the house. Tempered hardboard has been treated with special materials that make it quite hard as well as extra moisture-resistant, and it is used for bathroom and kitchen walls in place of expensive ceramic tile. However, it isn't necessary to spend the extra money for this material unless you really need the qualities built into it.

Store and protect board panels even more carefully than you would plywood. Use the same cutting procedure, too. In the case of pre-painted or plastic-covered boards, always score the decorative surface along the cut-line with a mason's knife before you begin to saw; this will minimize chipping.

Standard practice has been to use *plasterboard* for ceilings and walls, and to strip and plaster over perforated tape to achieve a perfect surface that looks like a skilled job of old-fashioned plasterwall. But such perfection is beyond the skill of most amateurs, so it's a much better bet to get a plasterer to put up the plasterboard. An even better bet is to do the best job you can and wallpaper over the plasterboard wall or install whatever plywood panels appeal to you. (See installation instructions in Chapter 6.)

You are probably quite familiar with *pegboard* (which will be discussed in the next chapter as a tool-holder). It has a series of evenly-spaced round holes or perforations across the surface. A wide variety of pre-formed hangers fit into these holes so that you can hang all sorts of objects ranging from pots and pans in the kitchen to hammers and saws in a workroom. Perforated hardboard or pegboard is available in either single or double thickness. Select the strength needed for the specific job.

For such use as storage, the material must be supported away from the wall about ½ inch to allow sufficient room for the various hooks to be inserted. Either frame the sheet or use the special spacer-blocks that are sold for this purpose by lumberyards and hardware stores.

Working with Plywood

Store large sheets in a cool, dry place. If you're going to have the material around for any length of time, it's a good idea to stack it flat where it won't come into contact with the weather. Make sure it is adequately supported so that the sheets won't sag.

Sawing

Always use a fine-tooth saw. (See illustration, Chapter 10, page 82.) If you are cutting by hand, that means a crosscut saw. Score the cutting-line with a mason's or carpenter's knife

before you saw to reduce splintering. Remember that there is a veneer on both sides of the sheet, so the scoring should be on both sides.

If you have power-tool equipment, use a special plywood-cutting blade on your saw. (See illustration, Chapter 5, page 35.) Mark your cut by scoring with a carpenter's square on both sides of the panel, precisely opposite on each side. Then adjust the cut of the power-saw so the blade just barely extends past the top of the sheet, reverse, and saw through the opposite side. If you lack the precision for this, saw through the underside of the sheet, remembering that your power-saw blade cuts downward. (If there is splintering, you want it on the back of the sheet.)

Normally, use thin plywood where the edges of the sheet can be fully supported by the work-table or by scrap-wood. For purposes such as doors, the panel plywood can be easily cut from both sides to the center, then planed.

A cabinet cannot, of course, be built entirely out of ¼-inch plywood, but requires a frame of solid-wood or heavier plywood to which you can fasten the plywood covering with glue, nails, or screws.

Acrylic Materials

More and more homeowners are discovering the delight of working with these twentieth-century materials, although they have become expensive during the oil crisis because they are petroleum-based. Acrylic material is crystal-clear and can be cut, bent, and cemented with amazing ease. Technically, Plexiglas is the brand name for one type of acrylic sheet. Lucite and corrugated plastic sheets are also among those used like wood. These rigid plastic materials are available in colorless form, and also in various transparent tints, translucent, and opaque colors, but should not be confused with other plastics. Safe to use, it is lightweight, not easily broken, and has good resistance to the weather. Incidentally, if you decide to work with Plexiglas, be sure to specify a type known as G. There is another variety known as K that is intended for safety-glazing as a replacement for glass. Type K cannot be cemented easily and is far more limited as a home-building material.

Like plywood, Plexiglas is available in a wide range of thicknesses as well as sheet-sizes. Your best bet is to make a sketch of the project you have in mind and then discuss the selection of material with the man behind the counter.

Working With Acrylics

The procedure for working with acrylics is pretty much the same as for working with wood or soft metal, except for a few aspects. The sheet, in a thickness of up to ¼ inch, can be scribed and snapped as you would a piece of glass. Use a straight-edge as a guide, and run the point of the special acrylic scribing tool down the sheet with firm pressure. You may have to repeat this procedure several times with thicker sheets. Slip a ¾-inch wooden dowel underneath the line of the intended break and press downward on either side with your hands.

The sheet can also be cut with a saw. Do not remove the protective masking-paper before you cut. Use a fine-tooth blade for the job. Hold the acrylic sheet down firmly, but don't force the saw. Power-equipment requires special blades for this material. Discuss the matter with your local lumber dealer or plastic supplier to make sure your power-saw is equipped with the proper blade for the job.

Drilling

Standard twist-drills work quite well with this material. Make sure that you back the sheet with a piece of wood, and clamp it or hold it down firmly. Use a rotary hand-drill or a slow-speed electric-drill. The bit must be sharp. Work with slow speed and minimum pressure. If you work too fast, you may find yourself in an unusual situation: Plexiglas and other acrylics have a tendency to climb the drill. Also, if too much pressure is used, you are likely to chip the material on the back-side.

Edge-finishing

There are three stages to edge-finishing: smooth finish, satin finish, and transparent finish. Here's the how-to of each one:

1. For a smooth finish that will remove the marks of the saw, merely scrape the edge with a sharp piece of metal such as the back of a hacksaw blade. Do not use the tooth side.
2. For satin finish, after scraping the edge as above, sand it with increasingly finer grits of wet-or-dry paper. Use the range from 150 to 320. Be careful not to round the edges.
3. For transparent finish, just keep sanding but work with even finer grits: use 400 to 500 wet-or-dry paper. After this, buff the edge using the special polishing kit intended for this material.

Heat-bending

You can easily bend the Plexiglas sheet along a straight line by using a strip-heater. This is an inexpensive gadget that you can buy with Plexiglas material. Remove the protective masking-paper and make a mark on the Plexiglas, using a china-marking pencil at the exact spot where you want the bend. Hold the Plexiglas section over the strip-heater. Heat the plastic until it softens in the area to be formed. This will take 5 or 6 minutes for ⅛-inch material, longer for thicker sheets.

Scribing and breaking acrylic sheet

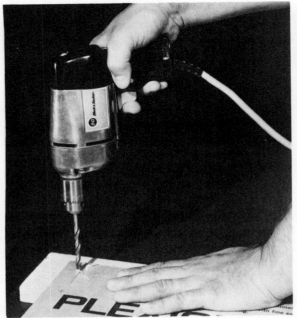

Drilling: acrylics may be drilled with a standard hand-drill at slow speed and light pressure, or at highest speed with an electric-drill with a high-speed twist-drill.

Strip heat-bending: acrylic sheets are bent with strip-heater. Work in well-ventilated area, never over an open flame, and with dry-powder fire-extinguisher nearby. Hold in desired position till cool.

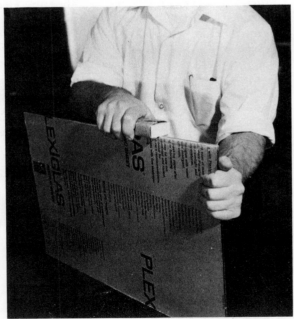

Edge-finishing: the edges are given a smooth finish by scraping with metal blade or by sanding with medium-grit paper (60–80). Sand with 150–320 grit paper for satin finish, which can be cemented or can be made transparent with 400–500 grit paper and buffed with fine grit compound.

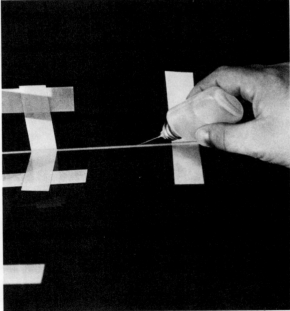

Cementing: Grade G (not K) acrylic is cemented with any of three solvents along satin-finish edges, joining them with strips of masking-tape until thoroughly dry.

With a gentle touch, bend the sheet to the desired angle and hold it firmly in this positon until it cools. For safety, do not overheat, work in a well-ventilated area, never bend over an open flame, and keep a dry-powder ABC fire-extinguisher nearby.

Cementing

With grade G acrylic material, this is a fast and easy job. Apply the special solvent-type adhesive evenly along the edges at satin finish edges to bind them into a seamless edge. The liquid will be drawn into the joint by capillary action. It will soften the edges of the sheets and, in effect, weld them together. Use the special applicator meant for this purpose. (It looks like a jumbo hypodermic needle.) The cement-joint must remain horizontal, held together with strips of masking-tape, until it has dried.

Acrylic Projects

A few projects that can be made from Plexiglas are a fish-tank and terrarium, a light-diffuser, a hanging partition, kitchen-cabinet sliding-panels, sliding doors, cube- and other occasional-tables, record-turntable covers, coasters, garden windbreaks, room-dividers, and display cases.

Nails, Screws, Bolts

You will, of course, save a great deal of time on incidental jobs if you buy an assortment of common nails, screws, and bolts, and put them in a row of glass jars on a shelf above your workbench. Many times, you may want two or three ordinary nails of a given length, and you can't go to the hardware store just for them. Most people have a tendency to put screws, bolts, small curtain fixtures, nuts, and all the rest in a box, canister, or jar, and are forced to dump everything out on a table or floor to find what they want. If you wish to do things right, your beginning collection should go into a small wooden cabinet especially made for it, with a series of three or four tiers of plastic drawers (transparent), graduated from small drawers on top for the smallest screws and tacks to a bottom row of largest drawers. But even with this, you may not have the in-

Apply weather stripping between plastic and frame of acrylic storm sash.

Acrylic storm-sashes; in some 30 states there are safety glazing laws and/or building-codes. When storm doors are broken, the householder can easily install acrylic sheets in place of glass, making allowance for a slight expansion.

triguing variety of metal objects in the large jar that will take you years to accumulate.

A crucial element in almost any home-building or repair project is how the various parts are held together. Most of the time this means either nails or screws. And yet few home-handymen bother to learn just how varied the assortment of types and sizes is. If you are willing to spend just a few moments of quick study you will be able to turn out much sturdier work and you will also save time.

Nails

The most common type of nail are just that — *common-nails*. These have large flat heads and are used for house-framing and most rough work.

For cabinet-work, *finishing-nails* are considerably thinner and have a much smaller head that is designed to be counter-sunk below the surface. *Box-nails* have the same general shape as common-nails, except they are much more slender and, as a result, less likely to split the wood. However, in driving into hard lumber, they do have a tendency to bend more easily. *Brads* (also known as wire-nails) are shaped like finishing-nails but are considerably finer.

In addition to these, there is a vast assortment of special nails made for specific jobs: *masonry-nails* (fat and incredibly tough) can actually be driven into cement; *scaffold-nails* (they have two heads so that the second one always projects up a bit from the surface making it easy to remove); *shingle-and-roofing nails* (for shingles and roofing, of course); *decorative-head nails* (to match wall-paneling) — the list is almost endless. Your best bet, if you have some special project in mind, is to look at the nail, screw, and bolt chart posted in every lumberyard and hardware store and ask the advice of the department chief. Take a copy of the chart home and become an expert in one easy lesson.

Nails are available with special coatings. These serve to make the fastener more rust-resistant or to give it greater holding-power. For example, *etched-nails* are considered to have almost three times the holding-strength of a smooth-shanked nail. *Cement-coated-nails* are at least twice as strong. *Hot-dipped-nails* are highly rust-resistant, and maintain a stronger than average grip on the wood-fibers.

Generally regarded as being top of the list are *ring-nails*. These have a series of raised projections circling the shank at several points. They hold fast with an incredible grip.

If splitting is a problem, don't expect to solve the hassle with a sharp nail. The fact of the matter is that a dull point works far better in going into wood without splitting it. You see, a sharp point pushes all the fibers to one side or the other as the nail enters. This gives wood a great tendency to split. A blunt point, on the other hand, will chew its way through the fibers. Old-time carpenters have a system when they run into a wood-splitting nail problem. They turn the nail upside down, rest the head against a firm surface and tap on the point a bit until it flattens and slightly mushrooms. When this nail is driven into the wood, it will generally go into place without splitting the wood. For some reason, a nail altered in this fashion is called a "Dutchman."

The size of nails is calculated by a very strange system originally based on the number of nails of one size that made up a pound. Because of the mushmouth tendency of the times, the term gradually got slurred into the word penny. For example, a ten-penny nail weighed 10 pounds per thousand nails. Since this word confusion took place in England, and since the English penny is abbreviated "d," the designation for a ten-penny nail even today is written 10d.

When you are buying nails, you have to specify the type (common, finishing, etc.), the size (or "d"), plus the coating, if any (hot-dipped, cement, etc.).

As you can see, for any unusual work this can become a little complicated. With your newly-acquired knowledge, hold a discussion with your friend behind the hardware counter. He can guide you in terms of what you need, but some specialty nails, although theoretically available, can be purchased only on special order, and this sometimes involves a long wait.

NAIL CHART

The chart below illustrates nails in most common usage. Most are available at your hardware dealer.

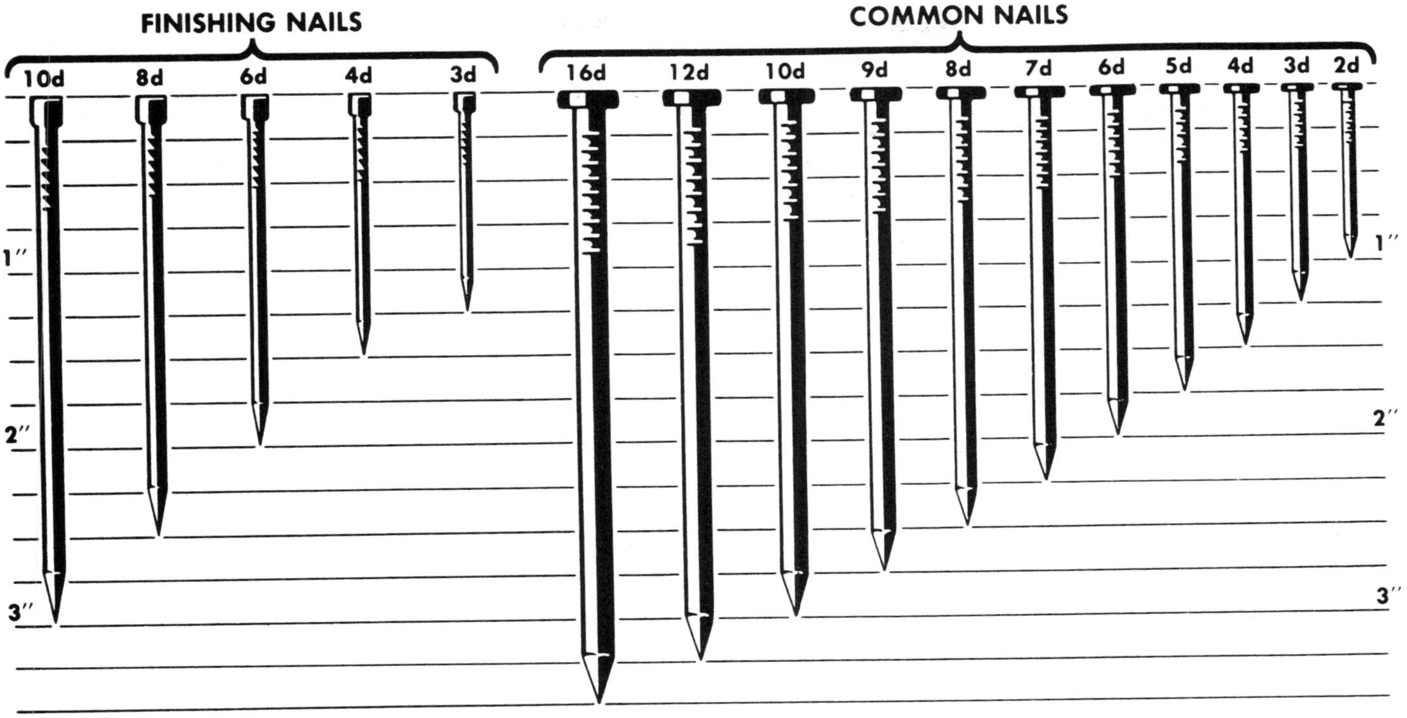
FINISHING NAILS
10d
8d
6d
4d
3d
COMMON NAILS
16d
12d
10d
9d
8d
7d
6d
5d
4d
3d
2d
1″
2″
3″

HOUSEHOLD NAILS

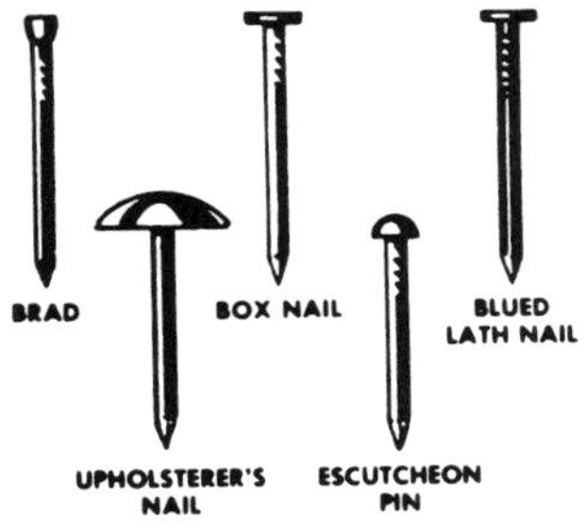
BRAD
BOX NAIL
BLUED LATH NAIL
UPHOLSTERER'S NAIL
ESCUTCHEON PIN

HOUSEHOLD TACKS

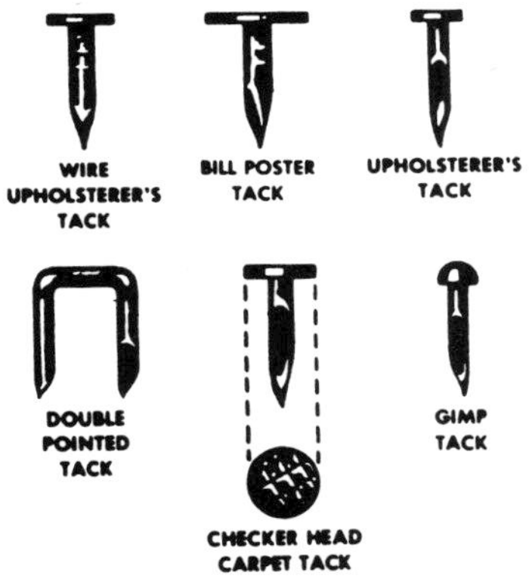
WIRE UPHOLSTERER'S TACK
BILL POSTER TACK
UPHOLSTERER'S TACK
DOUBLE POINTED TACK
CHECKER HEAD CARPET TACK
GIMP TACK

REFERENCE TABLE-COMMON NAILS

Size	Length and Gauge		Diameter Head	Approx. No. To Pound
2d	1 inch	No. 15	11/64	845
3d	1¼ inch	No. 14	13/64	540
4d	1½ inch	No. 12½	1/4	290
5d	1¾ inch	No. 12½	1/4	250
6d	2 inch	No. 11½	17/64	165
7d	2¼ inch	No. 11½	17/64	150
8d	2½ inch	No. 10¼	9/32	100
9d	2¾ inch	No. 10¼	9/32	90
10d	3 inch	No. 9	5/16	65
12d	3¼ inch	No. 9	5/16	60
16d	3½ inch	No. 8	11/32	45

REFERENCE TABLE-FINISHING NAILS

Size	Length and Gauge		Diameter Head Gauge	Approx. No. To Pound
3d	1¼ inch	No. 15½	12½	880
4d	1½ inch	No. 15	12	630
6d	2 inch	No. 13	10	290
8d	2½ inch	No. 12½	9½	195
10d	3 inch	No. 11½	8½	125

SCREW CHART

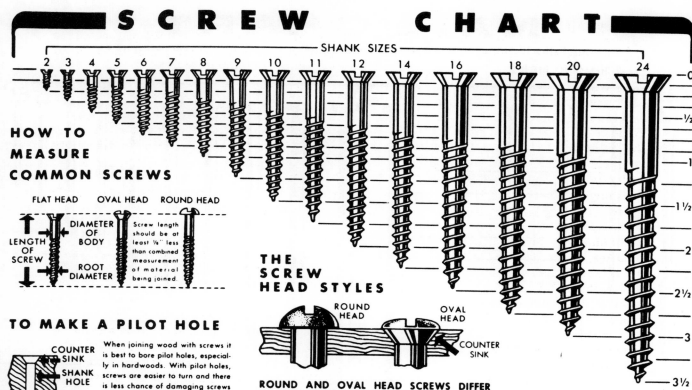

SHANK SIZES

2 3 4 5 6 7 8 9 10 11 12 14 16 18 20 24

0 — ½ — 1 — 1½ — 2 — 2½ — 3 — 3½

HOW TO MEASURE COMMON SCREWS

FLAT HEAD   OVAL HEAD   ROUND HEAD

LENGTH OF SCREW

DIAMETER OF BODY

ROOT DIAMETER

Screw length should be at least ⅛" less than combined measurement of material being joined.

TO MAKE A PILOT HOLE

COUNTER SINK
SHANK HOLE
PILOT HOLE

Pilot holes for small screws may be made with a brad awl, a gimlet or ice pick.

When joining wood with screws it is best to bore pilot holes, especially in hardwoods. With pilot holes, screws are easier to turn and there is less chance of damaging screws or wood. Bore holes large enough to easily accommodate screw shank in first piece of wood. Bore holes slightly smaller than thread diameters to a depth of half the length of threaded portion in second piece of wood. In hardwoods use a fine thread screw; in soft woods, use a coarse thread. Countersink to slightly less than diameters of screw heads.

THE SCREW HEAD STYLES

ROUND HEAD   OVAL HEAD   COUNTER SINK

ROUND AND OVAL HEAD SCREWS DIFFER FROM THE FLAT HEAD ONLY IN HEAD STRUCTURE. THE THREAD IS THE SAME. THEY ARE GENERALLY OBTAINABLE IN THE LENGTHS AND GAUGES CHARTED IN THE ABOVE DIAGRAM.

SHEET METAL SCREW STYLES

FLAT HEAD   OVAL HEAD   ROUND HEAD   BINDING HEAD

Two main types of Sheet Metal Screws are produced . . . Type A and Type B. Type A is intended for the joining or fastening of sheet metal 18 gauge or lighter. Type B is for use on sheet metal up to 6 gauge. Both types have the following head styles . . . Flat, Round, Oval, Binding and Stove. They are available in lengths from ⅛" to 2" and in these shank diameters . . . No's. 4, 6, 7, 8, 10, 12, 14. For best results, drilled or punched guide holes should be slightly smaller than screw diameter.

PHILLIPS SCREWS WITH RECESSED HEAD

PHILLIPS SCREW

This screw is best identified by the cross-shaped slot in the head. It is made in nearly as wide a range of sizes and gauges as the standard screw. It requires a special driver. Two sizes of Phillips Drivers fit the Phillips screws most often used.

PHILLIPS SCREW DRIVER

MAKE SCREW DRIVING EASIER FOLLOW THESE SUGGESTIONS

1 For easier driving, drill pilot holes . . especially in hardwoods.

2 Pick out a screw driver blade that seats snugly in the full width of the slot in the screw head.

3 Use as long a screw driver as possible; this gives greater leverage.

4 Keep driver square and flat in screw slot.

5 Hold driver in line with screw and apply steady, even pressure; hold screw with other hand until it is firmly started in the wood. Once started, most force is used to turn driver.

6 Seat screw firmly and snugly. Too much pressure can strip wood or break screw. (If pressure becomes too great before screw is fully driven, withdraw screw and rebore hole.)

Soaping or waxing threads on large screws makes them easier to drive.

Countersinking by use of auger bits is done to conceal screws with dowel pins or to extend screw deeper and more securely into material being joined.

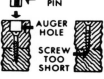

DOWEL PIN
AUGER HOLE
SCREW TOO SHORT

HOUSEHOLD SCREWS FOR SPECIAL USES

CUP HOOK   SCREW HOOK   "L" SCREW HOOK   SCREW EYE

THESE SCREWS ARE USUALLY AVAILABLE IN SEVERAL SIZES AND METALS

Wood-screws

There's an entirely different set of specifications and classifications for wood-screws. Here's how that situation is organized.

There are two types of slots cut in the top of the screw-head. The most familiar is the traditional straight-slot, but there's also a cross-slot — shaped like a plus-sign — called a Phillips head. The big advantage of this second variety is that the screwdriver does not have a tendency to slip out of the slot as it does with the straight variety,

The screw-head, when looked at in cross-section, comes in three different shapes. The most familiar is the flat-head. Just as the name indicates, the top surface of the screw is flat, and it tapers in an inverted cone to the shank or straight portion. In contrast, a round-head screw is dome-shaped on top but flat on the underside of the head. The third type is the type called an oval-head. It's slightly rounded on top and is tapered toward the shank.

Screws also vary according to the material used to make them, such as iron, brass, etc. There is also a variation according to any special treatments such as chrome-plating or paint.

As for size, there are two separate measurements. First is the gauge or screw-size, and this refers to the diameter of the screw-shank. In this classification, gauge No. 1 equals $1/16$ inch, and the sizes range up to No. 4 which equals $29/64$ inch. (See chart opposite.)

Length is measured in inches and fractions of an inch. The most commonly available lengths are ¼, ⅜, ½, ⅝, ¾, ⅞, and 1 inch. After 1 inch, the pattern shifts slightly and is 1¼, 1½, 1¾, 2, 2¼, 2½, 2¾, and 3. The next sizes are 4, 4¼, 5, and 6 inches.

The top portion of the screw is called the "head." The section underneath this, the smooth part before the threads begin, is called the "shank." Below this are the "threads," tapering down to the "points."

The length of a screw is calculated from the surface that will be flush with the surface of the wood to the end of the point. For a flat-head screw, the length is figured from the top of the head to the point. A round-head screw is calculated from the underside of the head to the point.

Not all sizes and gauges are available in all types of screws.

Putting all this together, a typical hardware-store conversation might go something like this. You walk into the store and you say, "Jack, I need a box of No. 4 flat-head Phillips bright-iron, ⅞-inch wood-screws." Jack may very well push a box of the exact hardware you ordered across the surface, but — the laws of supply and demand being what they are — it's more likely he'll counter your request with: "How about a straight slot?" or "Can you use 1-inch?" or "Would you mind if they're zinc-plated instead of bright-iron?" The moral is obvious: Ask for what you want but be prepared to compromise a bit.

To be properly installed, wood-screws require clearance-holes drilled in the wood. This is especially true in the case of hardwood. First, drill the hole for the shank of the screw. Since this doesn't involve any holding-power, the hole should be the same diameter as the screw-shank itself. Next, drill the hole below this for the threaded section. Since all the gripping-power comes from this area, the hole should be considerably smaller than the thread-portion of the screw. Finally, if you are using a flat- or oval-headed screw, counter-sink the cone-shaped hole at the top to take the screw-head. If a screw turns too hard, back it out and enlarge the pilot-hole for the threads a bit. At the same time you should scrape the threads of the screw across a bar of soap to make it easier to drive the screw into place.

Just as with nails and other types of fasteners, there are specialty screws intended for specific jobs. For example, there are jailhouse screws. These have a strange-looking slot cut into the head. Although they drive in place like conventional screws, it's impossible to back them out of the hole. If you really need any exotic items like this, you will probably have to ask your local store to special-order them.

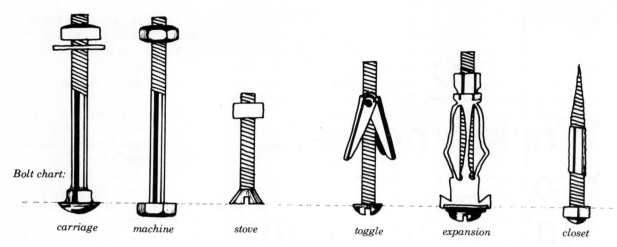

Bolt chart:

carriage   machine   stove   toggle   expansion   closet

Bolts

If you have the opportunity, visit rare specialty stores known to professional carpenters. There may be one in your city, and the experience is like going to a famous restaurant.

Though fewer in type, some of your worst problems can be solved by bolts: *carriage, stove, machine, closet, toggle,* and *expansion.* Togglebolts are used to attach fixtures to plasterwalls; expansion bolts are needed to fasten wood or other objects to masonry.

Corrugated Fasteners

The term "fasteners" is used for all such hardware as nails and bolts in somewhat the same way it is in the garment trade for zippers. Corrugated fasteners (see Chapter 4) should be used only in rather rough work, but you might find them skillfully fastening together the corners of picture-frames on the back-side.

12
Workbenches, Storage, and Maintenance of Tools

As you become involved in carpentry jobs, you will inevitably find that your assortment of tools will continually expand. Eventually, there will come a point where you need organized storage and work facilities.

Storage-panel and Safe-keeping

To keep tools conveniently at hand, put up a panel of peg-board. Lumberyards and supply companies, as well as many hardware stores, now sell a wide variety of hooks, clips, and fasteners designed to fit the holes in this material. You can hang your tools on this storage wall, where they will be readily accessible. To simplify the job of putting a tool back in a proper position, merely outline it on the board using a thick felt pen. Lost, strayed, or stolen can apply to tools more than any other kind of object. If you encase your peg-board and tool rack in thin plywood doors with a lock, you will not run the risk of mixing your tools with those of your helper. A large pipe wrench is much more costly than a chisel, yet it will invariably be the wrench that strays away. And you may not be using it nearly so often, so you will not miss it as quickly as you will the chisel. The outlines on the storage wall will remind you whether a tool has been left out, and it can be located immediately, before its whereabouts are forgotten.

This may sound like a great deal of work just to care for tools, but if the peg-board is put up when you acquire your first pliers, your additional tools will fall into place from the beginning, and not end up in a cardboard box in the basement, in the kitchen drawer, or in the closet. Or under a bush where you were pruning a branch last fall.

If you're going to be away for some time, rub a thin layer of paste wax on the exposed metal surfaces of your tools. When activity resumes, you can merely wipe down the tools with a dry cloth, and you're back in business.

For storage of small metal parts, such as curtain-rod fixtures, it's a good idea to pick up some sort of sizable metal container with a tightly-fitting lid. Many hardware stores sell rust-inhibiting paper or chemicals. You can line the inside of the container with the paper, or you can sprinkle the chemicals in the corners. Both are fairly effective and tend to ward off rust.

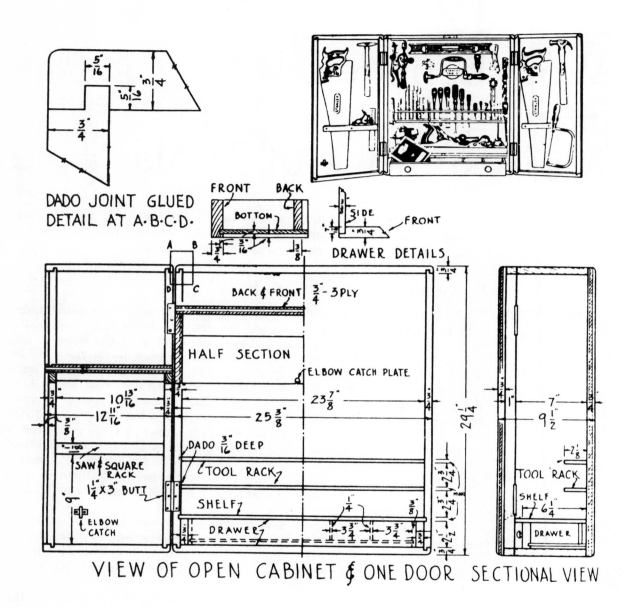

DADO JOINT GLUED
DETAIL AT A·B·C·D·

DRAWER DETAILS

VIEW OF OPEN CABINET & ONE DOOR   SECTIONAL VIEW

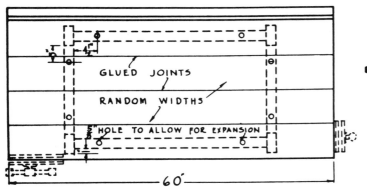

TOP VIEW

GLUED JOINTS

RANDOM WIDTHS

HOLE TO ALLOW FOR EXPANSION

60"

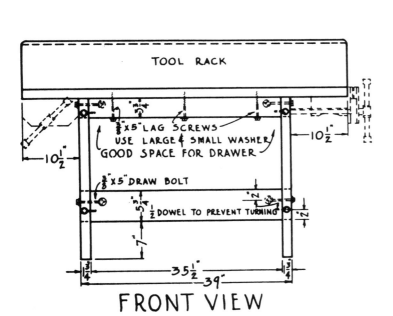

TOOL RACK

FRONT VIEW

$\frac{3}{8}$"X5" LAG SCREWS
USE LARGE & SMALL WASHER
GOOD SPACE FOR DRAWER

$\frac{3}{8}$"X5" DRAW BOLT

$\frac{1}{2}$ DOWEL TO PREVENT TURNING

35½"

39"

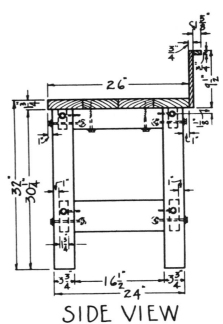

SIDE VIEW

26"

24"

16½"

Workmate: Sanding

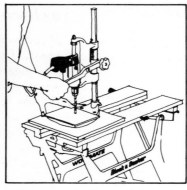
Drilling

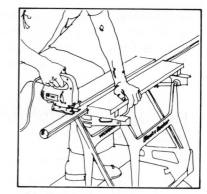
Pipe-cutting

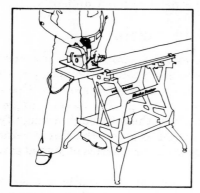
Sawing

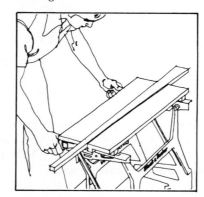
Vise for irregular wood

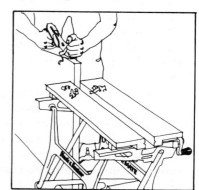
Vise for planing

Workbench and Accessories

For a workbench, there are no absolute rules except one: Do not try to get by with a discarded kitchen table; get an actual workbench that is sturdy, or make one. Build a rock-firm work-surface using such stock-size lumber as 2x4s or 2x6s. You may want to finish off the top-surface with a sheet of tempered Masonite. This hard, tough material will stand a great deal of pounding, but so will heavy wood.

You will soon want to add a vise to the workbench. For woodworking, get one with a convenient double-action screw mechanism. Pull the handle all the way open, and you can simply slide the jaws apart. Insert the work, push the jaws in place against it, and then turn the handle a few times for a firm grip. With this vise, you won't be screwing the jaws all the way in and out. Be sure that the jaws of the vise are lined with wood so that they won't damage your own wood.

A medium-size metal-working vise is quite useful, too, when fastened down to the surface of the workbench. Carpentry involves other materials in combination with wood. Select a metal vise with a swivel-base for greater versatility.

Workmate

Totally new in design, and extremely versatile, is a portable combination vise and work-surface called a "Workmate." It folds up so that you can carry it from one work-site to another. Opened out, it contains a series of adjustable V-grooves to grip tubular objects, a full-length vise to handle everything from small molding to a full-size door, plus pegs for irregular objects and adjustable-jaws to take wedge-shaped pieces. Quite sturdy, the rig even has a hold-down strut for your foot when you take on heavy-duty jobs. Adjustable legs provide a height of just under 2 feet or as much as 32 inches. If your space is limited, and if you can afford it, this may be your answer. You can carry it from a closet to a porch or bedroom (like a portable sewing-machine) and start work.

Handyman's Dream Workshop

There comes a time, at least for some people, when the special tool-shop has to be built, and the householder is capable of constructing it. The workshop illustrated here was worked out by the Stanley Tool Company in conjunction with *Popular Science* magazine. It is designed with a place for everything, from a tack to a shelf of paint-cans. The plans may be obtained from Stanley.

Two of the units (the middle two) are identical, as the plans show, and on the left is the cabinet for paints and drawers. By the time you have built this extraordinary piece of furniture, you will know exactly what each compartment is going to contain. The storage cabinet, only a foot deep, the same depth as the shelves and peg-board tool racks, can be locked for power-tools and spraying devices, which should remain safe and dust-free.

Surface Care of Metal Tools

Maintenance is a routine as easy as cleaning a razor, if you do it as you go. As you put it back, clean off each tool with a piece of cheesecloth or even an old undershirt. Wipe away the sawdust and dry the metal surfaces. Keep an oil rag conveniently nearby (free from spontaneous combustion) so that you can wipe off exposed metal to keep it from rusting. A good container for this is a one-pound tobacco jar. The lid will seal firmly so that you will not have a fire-hazard, and at the same time you will be able to open it without difficulty.

Sharpening Tools

Every cutting-tool, from the primitive savage's chipped-flint spear to the most precise scalpel, works in exactly the same way. Under close inspection, cutting-tools have a ragged appearance. Look at them through a magnifying glass. Even the edge on the finest razor-blades will appear to be a series of jagged saw-teeth.

That's how they cut. It's really a sawing-action. The big difference is that a properly sharpened blade will have much finer teeth, and so will appear to slice with infinite ease.

Handyman's dream-workshop: Pegboard cabinet sections; Drawer cabinet; Storage cabinet

Knives: To keep a knife-edge sharp and useful, use an oil-stone, the kind that has a medium grit on one side and fine on the other. An oil-stone is usually mounted in a wooden case. Fasten the case down to a work-surface or clamp it lightly in a vise to hold it in position while you work. Squirt a few drops of lubricating oil on the surface of the stone, and begin work on the coarse side. Sharpen the knife-blade by moving it away from you across the surface of the stone at a 15-degree angle. To determine sharpness, you'll have to feel along the side of the blade. The safe method is to slide your finger from the flat portion of the blade over the edge of it, rather than to risk a cut by running your finger along the edge. The testing motion is perpendicular to the blade.

Continue alternating forward and backward strokes of the blade, flipping it over each time until the feather-edge runs the full length of the blade. At this point, flip the stone over to the fine surface. Squirt a little more oil on it, and very lightly continue the same stroking pattern until you have removed the wire- or feather-edge.

If you are a stickler for a really fine job, you can finish the sharpening procedure by stropping the blade on a strip of leather. The easiest routine is to glue the leather down to a flat board. To strop the blade, start at the far end of the leather with the cutting-edge facing away from you. Pull the blade back toward you, then flip it over so the cutting-edge faces toward you, and push the blade across the strop away from you. (That's what the barber does with his old-fashioned straight-razor.) Maintain the same 15-degree angle during this maneuver.

Of course, if the blade is really hacked — that is, if you badly misused it, and there are deep nicks and gullies in the cutting-edge — this sharpening procedure is not enough to restore life. In such a case, you will have to grind the blade on a power-wheel. Since most home-workshops don't have a tool of this type, you are better off leaving the job to the professional grinder, and vowing to be more careful of the tool in the future.

Plane-blades

The professional procedure involves grinding the blade using a special guide hooked up to a power-grindstone. Since a precision-tool of this type is usually not included in a home-workshop assortment, you might seek professional help if your plane-blades are damaged beyond the remedy of simple flat-stone sharpening.

The angle of the plane-blade to the surface of

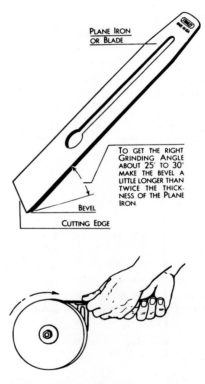

Grinding the plane-blade: The correct grinding angle of 25 to 30 degrees makes the bevel a little longer than twice the thickness of the plane-blade. Grinding straightens the edge and restores the bevel preparatory to sharpening by whetting on the oil-stone. The grindstone should turn toward the plane-iron and the blade should be moved from side to side. The guide assures a flat bevel. Keep the plane-blade cool by frequent dipping in water to prevent burning or softening of the steel.

the stone is very important. The blade should make a 25- to 30-degree angle with the surface.

Stop a moment to look at a plane-blade. You will notice that it has a bevel tapering down to the cutting-edge. Also, although you may not be able to see it with your naked eye, there is a second bevel. This one is much smaller and right next to the cutting-edge. It's the second bevel — the little one — that you want to sharpen. Here's how.

Don't try to hold the blade in your hand, or push it back and forth across the surface. Instead invest a small amount of money in a *plane-sharpening guide* (see illustration). This is a simple, inexpensive tool, which several manufacturers make. Although the mechanism may vary, they all work in the same way. You clamp the blade into the gadget and then adjust it so that it will hold the blade at the correct angle all the way across the sharpening stone.

You can, however, make the angle-adjustment by eye. First adjust the jig until the plane-blade sits flat on the larger bevel. Then raise it up just a little bit — no more than about 5 degrees — so that you'll be reinforcing the second bevel.

Squirt some oil on the stone, press down with moderate pressure, and slide the plane-blade along the stone. The cutting-edge should be facing away from you, and the movement of the blade across the stone should also be away from you. Lift the blade from the surface of the stone, bring it back to the starting point, and begin the next stroke. Stop every four or five strokes and feel the flat or upper surface of the blade. Gradually, a feather- or wire-edge should begin to form.

Use the same finger-testing routine as for the knife blade. In the interest of safety, stroke the upper or flat surface of the blade out across the edge. Do not run your fingers along the cutting-edge in a movement parallel to the newly-sharpened surface.

Turn the blade over so that the flat side of it rests on the stone. Hold it perfectly flat on the stone without any angle whatsoever. Again,

slide it across the stone with the cutting-edge facing forward. The purpose of this maneuver is to break off the tiny feather- or wire-edge that was formed by the first grinding.

If you do not have a grinding-stone, a plane-blade may be whetted to a sharp cutting-edge on an oil-stone. This is a much simpler operation.

Hold the plane-iron or blade in the right hand, with the left hand helping. Place the bevel on the stone, with the back-edge slightly raised — at the 25- to 30-degree level — and move the plane-iron back and forth.

To keep the bevel straight, be sure the hands move parallel to the stone so that the angle between the plane-iron and the stone will stay the same throughout the stroke. Use enough oil to keep the surface of the stone moist. It keeps the stone sharp by preventing particles of steel from filling the pores of the stone. Try to wear the stone evenly.

Remove the wire- or feather-edge by taking a few strokes with the flat side of the plane-iron held *flat* on the stone. Avoid creating the slightest bevel on this side. If a nick or a shiny edge of bluntness can be seen, repeat both processes of whetting.

To finish the job, turn the stone over so that the fine surface faces up. Squirt some oil on it, and repeat the procedure.

Finish with a few strokes on a leather strop to produce a keener edge.

This is the craftsman's method. In the opinion of professional carpenters, it is the only way to sharpen a plane-blade. However, there

Chisels can be sharpened with a fine file.

may be times when you prefer a quick unprofessional method that is not as good but is at least serviceable. Let's say that you are working outside, intent on finishing a job before darkness closes in. You are smoothing the edge of a board when suddenly, zing, you run into a nail that was hidden just below the surface. As a result, there is now a slight nick in the plane-blade. If you go back to the workbench and dig out the necessary equipment, the proper grinding procedure may take a half-hour or more.

Instead, using a fine file, work very carefully across the cutting-bevel in a side-to-side motion, removing enough material to eliminate the nick. Turn the blade over, and use the file flat on the back-surface to remove the feather-edge. (Other tool-blades are normally sharpened with a file.)

Granted, the sharpening job will not be as good. You'll probably have to sharpen the plane-blade again in the proper manner (using an abrasive stone) before you can get full utility out of it. But, with this procedure, you will be able to finish your project without delay.

Chisel

The procedure with a chisel is very much the same as that followed for a plane-blade. Clamp the chisel in a guide, adjust it until the bevel is flat on the stone, and then crank up the guide about 5 degrees more. Use the same back-and-forth routine with both sides of the blade, until you have a well-honed cutting-edge.

A good filing will serve well on a chisel-blade. Admittedly, such a procedure is on the rough-and-ready side, but it's handy when you don't have a grinding-wheel, and some craftsmen are most skilled with it.

Screwdrivers

Surprisingly enough, these tools need occasional sharpening, too. Clamp the blade, tip-side up, in a sturdy vise. Using a fine or medium flat file, square off the tip by filing across the metal in a direction away from you. Be very careful to keep the file absolutely flat. If you rock it during the stroke, you will round the tip of the screwdriver-blade. The result is, in the language of New England carpenters, a disbenefit.

If the tip of the blade is twisted, you are using a poor-quality screwdriver or a blade that is too small for the screw-slot, or you are applying too much muscle. You may be able to clear up the distorted metal with a file, unless the damage is too great. In this case, get a new tool. You cannot merely keep grinding until you get down to undamaged metal. The tip of a good-quality screwdriver has been hardened in a very precise pattern. Too much filing or grinding will reach untempered metal that will twist out of shape the very first time you use it.

Index